DISASTER MITIGATION
A Community Based Approach

Development Guidelines, No 3
(Series Editor: Brian Pratt)

Andrew Maskrey

© Oxfam, 1989

British Library Cataloguing in Publication Data

Maskrey, Andrew *1957—*
  Disaster mitigation: a community based approach. (Development Guidelines)
  1. Developing countries. Disaster relief
  I. Title II. Series
  363.3'48'091724

ISBN 0 85598 122 9
ISBN 0 85598 123 7 pbk

Published by Oxfam, 274 Banbury Road, Oxford OX2 7DZ
Designed by Oxfam Design Studio
Printed by Oxfam Print Unit
Typeset in 11 point Garamond

Contents

Foreword   v
Introduction   vii
Acknowledgements   ix

Part 1 Vulnerability to disaster

Chapter One Approaches to vulnerability   1
Chapter Two Seismic vulnerability in metropolitan Lima   5
Chapter Three Huaicos and floods in the Rimac Valley, Peru   13
Chapter Four Vulnerability in other contexts   25

Part 2 Disaster mitigation

Chapter Five Approaches to mitigation   39
Chapter Six Lima's seismic protection plan   41
Chapter Seven Rimac Valley project   47
Chapter Eight The recovery of Cuyocuyo   63
Chapter Nine Mitigation programmes in other contexts   69
Chapter Ten Implementing community based mitigation   91

Further Reading   100

Foreword

Some months ago, I had the privilege of reading the final drafts of this extremely important book - one of the first to my knowledge, to focus on the actual experience of a community responding to a severe natural hazard that threatened their lives and property with detailed and ambitious mitigation action. As I read the text, I was reminded of a pair of memorable conversations, each reflecting a very different view of the world.

In 1972, I embarked on research into post-disaster emergency shelter needs and provision. One of the first pieces of advice I received came in Columbus, Ohio, from two eminent professors in the Disaster Research Centre , Henry Quarantelli and Russell Dynes. "We must warn you at the outset of your travels that in our experience you will hear a gross exaggeration of damage and casualties from disaster impact and an even grosser underestimate of local resources to tackle the problems of disaster victims." Their wisdom related to post-disaster recovery - but later it became clear that their perception was also widely applicable to pre-disaster preventive measures.

In the subsequent years, field study in various places continually reaffirmed their experience and there was no better evidence than this than at a highly influential conference held in Jamaica in 1981 to discuss the implementation of Disaster Mitigation Measures. What became clearly apparent as the meeting progressed was a situation where we were long in ideas, recommendations and advice whilst practical experience remained exceedingly short. Thus case studies of implementation were gold dust and one field report that sticks firmly in my memory is that of Andrew Maskrey, which has been expanded in this publication.

During his presentation I sat next to a delegate from the Middle East. He was in a very senior position in a Government Ministry with a specific concern for earthquake reconstruction planning that incorporated mitigation measures. He became increasingly restive during Andrew's talk of mobilisation of the community to map hazards, construct protective walls etc. Then as we left the meeting he placed his hand on my shoulder and shook it vigorously - "What on earth," he asked, "are these people and that speaker's organisation doing? It is clearly the Peruvian government's job to protect its citizens - not to leave it to the erratic performance of non-governmental agencies, who lack the necessary resources." I responded with the rather unoriginal comment that governments in all countries are overstretched in terms of cash, manpower skills and expertise and should therefore only commit their resources to what communities are unable to do. Therefore, if the occupants of this highly dangerous valley were both willing and capable of introducing protective measures - surely this should be applauded and not condemned. We went on to debate the side-benefits such as the development of local institutions and the potential value of this experience in terms of raising the perception of flood risk within the entire community by this form of social mobilisation. He remained singularly unconvinced, trapped by a deep conviction about the virtues of centralisation of power in governments and a paternalistic confidence (probably based more on hope than experience) in the ability of governments to act effectively and a corresponding mistrust of local communities.

Therefore this book contains a series of vital lessons that can be drawn about the opportunities and constraints on local communities to instigate protective action and as such is a commentary on a fundamental issue of development. Disaster Mitigation (as Jo Boyden from OXFAM observed in a thoughtful editorial of a few years ago) is essentially the transfer of power, as it increases the: "self-reliance of people in hazard-prone environments - to demonstrate that they have the resources and organisation to withstand the worst effects of the hazard to which they are vulnerable. In other words, disaster mitigation - in contrast to dependence-creating relief is empowering." [1]

As disaster risks increase due to urbanisation, deforestation and population growth pressures, concerned officials in government or voluntary agencies will be wise to reflect on lessons from the Peruvian experiences described so vividly in this book. The community based approach may be the only way forward given the frequent pattern of governmental apathy towards their poor citizens and the limitations of overstretched public sectors.

Ian Davis,
Chair, Disaster Management Centre,
Oxford Polytechnic.

---

[1] BOYDEN, Jo, DAVIS, Ian, Editorial: Getting Mitigation on the Agenda. Need this Happen?, Special Issue of Bulletin 18, University of Reading Agricultural Extension and Rural Development Centre, October 1984, P.2.

Introduction

Background

This book recounts the author's experiences of a number of disaster mitigation programmes developed in Peru. The author worked as a planner in a government agency, INADUR, Instituto Nacional de Desarollo Urbano (National Institute of Urban Development) between 1981 and 1983 and was founder member and co-director of a national non-governmental organisation (NGO), PREDES, Centro de Estudios y Prevencion de Desastres (Disaster Prevention and Research Centre) until 1985. The book argues in favour of a community based approach to disaster mitigation, and is aimed at those who work in NGOs, international development agencies or government departments.

Between 1982 and 1983, INADUR produced an innovative earthquake vulnerability study and protection plan for the metropolitan area of Lima-Callao. It was one of the first systematic studies of this kind to be carried out in a Latin American city. At the same time it adopted an alternative approach, looking at vulnerability not as a characteristic of earthquake but of the urbanisation process. The mitigation measures proposed focused on policy changes and legal and financial measures designed to avoid the emergence of vulnerable conditions rather than just on physical measures to reinforce houses and buildings.

PREDES, formed by three members of the INADUR team, set up a community based mitigation programme in 1983 in the Rimac Valley, east of Lima. The valley is one of the most disaster prone areas in Peru, suffering annual floods, as well as landslides and earthquakes. The programme enabled communities to implement their own mitigation programmes through: a) strengthening community organisation; b) providing technical assistance and training; c) developing mitigation proposals which communities could negotiate with government or international agencies. The experience allowed PREDES to advise NGOs working in other disaster areas: in Colcabamba, Huancavelica and in Cuyocuyo, Puno. However, when the experience was presented in international forums (in Bolivia, India and Jamaica) it was realised that the methodology of community based mitigation could be valuable for other groups working in various contexts.

The conclusions and lessons from the INADUR and PREDES programmes have been compared with documented case studies of disasters in other countries, mainly from Latin America. The risks of analysing material from secondary sources are considerable and are fully recognised here. Nonetheless, the conclusions of other programmes are remarkably coherent with those of the Peruvian cases and add further weight and evidence to the arguments in favour of community based disaster mitigation.

The conclusions reached are necessarily provisional and need to be verified in the light of further experience. There are still very few examples of community based mitigation programmes. It is hoped that this book will stimulate new practice, encourage the sharing of information between those involved and lead to the setting up and evaluating of more community based mitigation programmes. In this way, the roles and responsibilities for mitigating disasters may come to be redefined.

Structure of the book

The book is in two parts. Part I looks at vulnerability to disaster. Chapter 1 reviews existing theories to identify two different approaches to interpreting vulnerability. Two in-depth case studies then examine vulnerability to different hazards. Chapter 2 examines seismic vulnerability in Lima and Chapter 3 is concerned with vulnerability to floods and alluvions in the Rimac Valley. Chapter 4 consists of a comparative analysis of documented case studies on vulnerability in different contexts and presents conclusions and reflections on the evidence accumulated as to the causes and evolution of vulnerability.

Part II looks at ways of mitigating disaster. Again, hypotheses are established and examined through case studies leading to conclusions. Chapter 5 discusses the conventional top down approach to mitigation, its limitations and the case for community based protection. Chapter 6 gives an account of the Seismic Protection Plan for Lima. Chapter 7 is a detailed case study of community based mitigation carried out in the Rimac Valley, and an evaluation of the project. Chapter 8 is another case study of successful community based risk-reduction, in Cuyocuyo. Chapter 9 is a comparative analysis of documented case studies on both top down and community based programmes from other contexts and presents conclusions on these two mitigation models. Chapter 10 gives guidelines for NGOs wishing to encourage community based mitigation and establishes a number of priorities and principles for successful implementation. Finally, an agenda for the agencies is suggested.

Acknowledgements

This work has been carried out with the financial support of OXFAM, who also sponsored the PREDES programme. Ian Davis of the Disaster Management Centre at Oxford Polytechnic gave considerable encouragement to write up the case studies and both he and Yasemin Aysan read through the drafts. Both Christine Whitehead and Marcus Thompson at OXFAM and Ian Davis gave access to the set of case study material, which has been analysed here. The research and writing was carried out in AHAS (Associated Housing Advisory Services) a London based NGO of which the author is a member. John and Bertha Turner of AHAS both commented on the draft. The Disaster Mitigation Workshop held at Habitat Forum Berlin in June 1987 provided a further opportunity to discuss the cases and draw conclusions, with colleagues from Peru, El Salvador and Mexico.

Josefa Rojas, who worked in PREDES from 1983 to 1985 and who jointly organised the Disaster Mitigation Workshop in Berlin worked as co-researcher on the case studies from other contexts. Her thesis "El Papel del Trabajo Social en la Prevencion de los Desastres: El Caso del Valle Rimac - The Role of Social Work in Disaster Prevention: the Case of the Rimac Valley" (Universidad Catolica del Peru, 1986) together with the book "Urbanizacion y Vulnerabilidad Sismica en Lima Metropolitana - Urbanisation and Seismic Vulnerability in Metropolitan Lima" (Maskrey, A, Romero, G, PREDES, 1986) provided the starting point for the present paper.

Finally, thanks are expressed to community leaders and residents of the Rimac Valley, Peru, who are the real authors of the ideas expressed here as well as to all those who worked in or collaborated with PREDES in the development of its projects.

Effect of mudslide, Chosica, Rimac Valley.

Dave Eminson/Oxfam

PART ONE

VULNERABILITY TO DISASTER

Chapter One

APPROACHES TO VULNERABILITY

Disaster and Vulnerability

Natural hazard and natural disaster are two very different terms which are frequently confused and used interchangeably. Earthquake, flood, and cyclone come to be synonymous with disaster but, although natural hazards like earthquakes can be highly destructive, they do not necessarily cause disaster. An earthquake in an uninhabited desert cannot be considered a disaster, no matter how strong the intensities produced. An earthquake is only disastrous when it directly or indirectly affects people, their activities and their property.

Natural disasters are generally considered as a coincidence between natural hazards (such as flood, cyclone, earthquake and drought) and conditions of vulnerability. There is a high risk of disaster when one or more natural hazards occur in a vulnerable situation:

RISK = VULNERABILITY + HAZARD

The United Nations Commission for Human Settlements (UNCHS - HABITAT) has defined the three terms in the following way:[1]

HAZARD - is the probability that in a given period in a given area, an extreme potentially damaging natural phenomena occurs that induces air, earth or water movements, which affect a given zone. The magnitude of the phenomenon, the probability of its occurrence and the extent of its impact can vary and, in some cases, be determined.

VULNERABILITY - of any physical, structural or socioeconomic element to a natural hazard is its probability of being damaged, destroyed or lost. Vulnerability is not static but must be considered as a dynamic process, integrating changes and developments that alter and affect the probability of loss and damage of all the exposed elements.

RISK - can be related directly to the concept of disaster, given that it includes the total losses and damages that can be suffered after a natural hazard: dead and injured people, damage to property and interruption of activities. Risk implies a future potential condition, a function of the magnitude of the natural hazard and of the vulnerability of all the exposed elements in a determined moment.

[1] UNCHS, Settlement Planning for Disasters, Nairobi, 1981

Two Approaches to Vulnerability

Most work on vulnerability has been done during the last decade, although researchers have been looking at the causes of natural disasters for a great deal longer. Two opposing approaches emerge from the disaster equation presented above. Most research has taken as its starting point the assumption that disasters are characteristics of natural hazards. A small but significant body of research, however, has argued instead that disasters are characteristics not of hazards, but of socioeconomic and political structures and processes. These two approaches have been labelled as the "dominant" approach and the alternative "political economy" approach.[2] The second approach has emerged to a certain extent as a critique of the first. It seems useful to consider the two approaches as ends of a wide spectrum, containing a range of viewpoints and options, rather than as opposed positions.

At one extreme of the spectrum, the perception is that disasters are irrevocably caused by the impact of natural hazards on people and their activities. Disaster is perceived as an accident; as an unforeseen consequence of unpredictable and uncertain natural forces; as an inevitable occurrence. Research centres on the characteristics of the hazards themselves and attempts to predict their magnitude and occurrence through sciences such as seismology and meteorology.

Towards the centre of the spectrum, much research by the different technical professions shows that different kinds of construction and settlement patterns receive different impacts from hazards with the same characteristics and of a similar size. Research focuses on physical vulnerability to different hazards, identifying the resistance of different structures and materials in different kinds of locations. Much vulnerability analysis is of this kind.

Hand in hand with this research, the human ecology of hazards has emerged. It attempts to explain the differential effects of hazards not only on physical structures but on people, their economic activities and social relationships

Vulnerability is examined through concepts such as maladaptation, the inability to incorporate hazards within living patterns and irrational human response to hazard. The common element, which links all these

---

[2] WINCHESTER, P, Vulnerability and Recovery in Hazard Prone Areas, Middle East and Mediterranean Regional Conference on Earthen and Low Strength Masonry Buildings in Seismic Areas: Middle East Technical University, Ankara, Turkey, August 1986.

levels of analysis and which gives the dominant approach its coherence, is the perception of disaster as a characteristic of hazard. Disaster is seen as a function of hazard which, as causal agent, acts on passive, vulnerable conditions. Everyday life is considered to be normal and undisastrous. Only with the interruption of an unscheduled hazard does disaster occur.

At the other end of the spectrum, if vulnerability is seen as the effect of social and economic processes, some intrinsic flaws in the dominant approach can be demonstrated. In the dominant approach, it is supposed that people live in vulnerable conditions because of their own lack of knowledge about hazards or their erroneous perceptions of risk or because of inefficient decision-making and management structures in their society. However, the approach is unable to explain how individual decisions are affected or influenced by social and economic constraints. Numerous case studies now show that individuals or social groups may have very little freedom to choose how and where they live. For example, low income groups often have no choice except vulnerable locations, such as flood plains, for settlement. This is not due to lack of knowledge or an inefficient land use planning system but to the control of land by market forces, which does not allow low income groups access to safe building land.

The starting point of the political economy approach is that hazards are normal physical characteristics of the areas where they occur. Vulnerability is consequent not on hazard but on particular social, economic and political processes. Disaster is an extreme situation which results from these processes.

Unlike the dominant approach, the alternative political economy approach provides an analysis capable of addressing social process, organisation and change. Large numbers of people on the social and territorial periphery of the global economic and political system are seen to be disabled by unequal economic relationships which do not allow them access to the basic resources, such as land, food and shelter, necessary to stay alive. The empirical evidence, from a large number of case studies, points to the fact that it is these groups who most often suffer disaster. Vulnerable conditions are far more prevalent in the Third World than in the First World.

The gradual evolution of thinking and research away from the dominant approach towards the alternative political economy approach, has brought with it a new danger. In the analysis of global social and economic process, there is a tendency to lose sight of the local specificity of vulnerability in areas which suffer different hazards.

This book maintains that the analysis of specific risks to a given hazard and the analysis of socioeconomic processes are not mutually incompatible. Indeed, the experiences which will be presented show that both levels of analysis are necessary to explain people's vulnerability and their actions in the context of that vulnerability.

The way in which vulnerability arises and is perceived will be examined through two detailed case studies based on first hand experience: seismic vulnerability in Lima, Peru and floods and huaicos in the Rimac Valley, Peru.

Map showing Rimac river and valley, Peru.

Chapter Two

SEISMIC VULNERABILITY IN METROPOLITAN LIMA

Introduction

On 24 May 1940 an earthquake hit Lima leaving 179 people dead and 3,500 injured. Studies carried out in 1983 showed that if an earthquake of similar intensity occurred again, there would be far greater damage to buildings and many more people would be killed and injured. This case study shows that Lima's vulnerability has increased because of the way the city and its buildings have developed and been transformed as part of wider social processes.

Earthquakes in Lima

Lima is located on the Pacific coast of Peru, where two tectonic plates known as the Nazca and Americana Plates come into contact. The movement of the Nazca Plate pushing underneath the Americana Plate causes considerable seismic activity in the area. Until the end of the 19th century no less than 2,500 earthquakes were recorded in Peru. The most important earthquakes to shake Lima occurred in 1687, 1746, 1940, 1966 and 1974.

It is still impossible to predict when and where future strong earthquakes will occur on the Peruvian coast; at best, one can only speak of probabilities. Enrique Silgado in a book *Terremotos en el Peru*, written together with Alberto Giesecke in 1980, has estimated that, over a 100 year period, the probability of an 8.6 Richter earthquake occurring is 96%. In other words, being in a zone of high seismic activity, one day another strong earthquake will inevitably occur.

Vulnerability to Earthquakes

Damage in the earthquakes varied in similar structures in different areas, depending on variations in soils and geology. There are many factors which affect the number of deaths and the amount of destruction caused by an earthquake. In buildings, the materials used, the structure, the height and the level of deterioration are all important variables. How dangerous a particular neighbourhood is will depend on the availability of open space, the width of the streets, the number of access routes and building density. Other factors to be considered are population density and the ability of people to escape and deal with an emergency, which depends in turn on training and organisation. Income and occupational structures also affect vulnerability. Poor people have more difficulty in recovering from a disaster especially if their livelihood is affected. Seismic vulnerability is determined by a complex interplay of all the above factors.

In Lima, three broad patterns of seismic vulnerability can be identified. In residential areas developed by the private sector or government agencies for middle and high income groups, vulnerability is relatively low. Buildings are generally well constructed, complying with building regulations and incorporating antiseismic structures. Population densities are low. There is open space and broad streets. If affected by an earthquake people's incomes give them a better chance of recovery from disaster.

In the new settlements (pueblos jovenes) on the city periphery, seismic vulnerability is also fairly low. Housing is either built from lightweight materials such as bamboo, or else has fairly solid brick construction with reinforced concrete columns. Population densities again are low. If people are affected, their low incomes are a handicap, but on the other hand possibilities of recovery are enhanced by a

Penny Tweedie/Oxfam

Houses in the pueblos jovenes on the city periphery are often built of lightweight materials like bamboo. In the event of an earthquake, although the houses might be destroyed, the death rate would be relatively low, in contrast to the inner slum areas.

generally high level of organisation.

It is in the inner city slum areas that seismic vulnerability is highest. Houses are built from adobe, a material with little seismic resistance. Structures have been weakened by deterioration and the effects of earlier earthquakes. There is an absence of open spaces and escape routes and streets are narrow. Buildings are multioccupied with severe overcrowding. Organisation is almost non-existent and most families have low and irregular incomes. People in these areas are most likely to suffer disaster and least able to recover. The situation in some inner city pueblos jovenes is also critical.

The most critical areas in Lima are those slum areas which, because of underlying soils and geology, experience high seismic intensities. Studies have predicted that in the event of an earthquake of magnitude 8.2 Richter, over 26,000 dwellings would be destroyed or made unusable and about 128,000 people would be left homeless in these areas

Seismic Vulnerability and Urbanisation

Urban systems as a whole and cities in particular grow up as a result of complex economic and social forces and relationships. The formation of Lima on the Peruvian coast at the mouth of the river Rimac corresponded to changes in the Peruvian economy brought about by the Spanish conquest. Under the Incas all the agricultural and mineral surplus produced was concentrated in highland cities like Cuzco in the southern Andes. This urban system was integrated internally by a network of roads which linked all parts of the empire to its principal urban centre - the residence of the Inca and a military and theocratic elite.

After the destruction of Inca society by the invaders and the incorporation of Peru into a new political and economic structure based on the relationship with Spain, a radically different urban system emerged. New settlements were formed in the interior for colonial administration and to extract minerals. The most important cities were built on the coast to ship Peru's mineral wealth to Spain and to import consumer products for the new elite. Movement was from the interior to the coastal cities and there was no need for cities within the country to interrelate. Principal cities such as Lima, Arequipa and Trujillo were largely isolated from each other. The decision to locate Lima and other large cities on the Peruvian coast was based on new economic, political and administrative needs and earthquake risk was not a consideration.

The replacement of Spanish colonialism by British commercial interests after independence in 1832 tended to reinforce this territorial structure. The successive exploitation of guano, rubber, sugar, cotton and wool was intensified, while the internal market was flooded with cheap manufactured products. Although Lima was the political and administrative capital its influence extended little beyond its own hinterland, and it remained unconnected to the other principal urban centres.

The great depression of the 1920s and the Second World War were events which led to a process of industrialisation in Lima. The war interrupted the importing of manufactured products and created conditions for the development of industrial growth based on import-substitution. In the 1950s the manufacturing sector achieved a higher percentage of the Gross Domestic Product than the agricultural sector for the first time. The increase in trade, the growth of public administration, the construction of new roads, the enlargement of the consumer market, and industrial development itself were factors which determined the rapid growth of Lima and Callao, its port, and their consolidation as a dominant urban centre which integrated the whole country in economic and territorial terms. An enormous wave of migration occurred to the major cities and especially to Lima.

Between 1940 and 1981, the percentage of the population of Peru living in cities grew from 34.8% to 65.1%. In that time the population of Lima-Callao grew from 645,172 to 4,608,010, and it now has over 27% of the country's population and 70% of the industry. The concentration of population in one capital city and the impoverishment and relative depopulation of rural areas has been a feature of the changing economic structure in many countries over the same period. The occurrence of destructive earthquakes on the Peruvian coast was not a factor which carried any weight in the growth of Lima. Obviously, vulnerability to earthquakes increases dramatically as population, activities and buildings become concentrated in areas which experience high seismic intensities.

Form of Building and Settlement

The form of building and settlement which has accompanied urban growth is also an important factor in determining vulnerability. The Spanish form of building, with adobe walls and heavy tiled or mud roofs, was not seismic resistant - originating as it did in a region which seldom experiences earthquakes. Under Spanish rule, the same planning and building forms spread throughout the country. The successive destructions of Lima by earthquakes in 1586, 1655, 1687,

1746 and 1828 demonstrated the inherent vulnerability of the building form.

In terms of building form Lima has probably become less vulnerable since the 1940s, as new building has used brick and reinforced concrete and has taken into account earthquake risk, although, as experiences in Mexico have shown, much apparently safe building can prove to be defective and dangerous in the event of an earthquake.

The Transformation of the City

The expansion of Lima since 1940 can be explained as a result of the varying objectives and actions of different social groups - a wave of migrants hoping to guarantee their livelihood in the city and a powerful elite sector made up of landowners, the construction industry and financiers, who have controlled and exploited resources such as land, building materials and finance for profit. With varying success, the Government has tried to coordinate and complement the workings of urban capital through special financial mechanisms, land use planning and direct housing construction using public funds and international loans. The Government also legalised the occupation of marginal land by low income groups and promoted progressive self-help building as a way for low income groups to solve their housing problems.

With the establishment of industrial, commercial and service activities in the traditional residential areas of the centre of Lima and Callao, Lima's wealthy families moved out to establish new middle class suburbs. At the same time, while trying to obtain a foothold in the urban economy, migrants occupied cheap rented rooms in areas close to concentrations of urban services. The large houses of the old families were subdivided and rented out to migrants. In the same areas, empty lots were used to build workers' houses specifically for renting. Other families built their own shacks in vacant areas.

Slum housing helped people to become established in the city. It was cheap, gave good accessibility to work and services and was temporary. While slum dwellers are well aware of earthquakes and even have an earthquake saint, which is carried in procession through Lima's streets every October, earthquake risk was not a factor which influenced migrants' decisions to live in the slums. For families with low incomes, the positive factors were of more importance. For many, living in a slum was the only option open.

Since the 1950s, organised groups of families from the slums invaded marginal desert and hills at the edge of the city to build pueblos jovenes. In the inner city slums there was a fairly rapid population turnover as migrants became established in the city and looked to the pueblos jovenes to improve their housing situation.

In the 1970s, new factors intervened in this process. Marginal land became more scarce and, as new pueblos jovenes were further and further away from the city, costs increased and advantages decreased for slum dwellers thinking of moving out. With the economic crisis of the 1970s, the number of people working in unstable 'survival' activities increased rapidly and for them the accessibility factor became all important. Building costs increased far faster than real incomes, and consequently the possibilities for self-help building were considerably reduced.

These and other factors meant that population turnover in slum areas stagnated. What was temporary housing became permanent. Older pueblos jovenes with a high population density have become new slum areas. Increased demand for cheap rented housing in central areas has caused the saturation of existing slum areas and overcrowding in new areas. The availability of cheap rented housing in the older areas has actually decreased as slums have been demolished and residents evicted to make way for more profitable uses and new blocks of flats, offices or shops have been built on the cleared sites.

In the slum areas of Lima, the population living in old adobe and quincha buildings has increased 30 or 40 fold in this century, giving rise to an unprecedented increase in the city's vulnerability. The formation of slums cannot be explained in isolation. It is characteristic of an urbanisation process in which land, building materials and finance are under the control of a small, powerful group, within the context of a political and socioeconomic structure dominated by national and international market forces.

Deterioration of Buildings

For many low income families there is no alternative to living in overcrowded conditions in areas which experience high seismic intensities. However, their vulnerability is further increased through the deterioration of the buildings.

Two factors play a key role in the deterioration of buildings: overuse and lack of maintenance. A building deteriorates more rapidly if it is submitted to intensive and inappropriate use and if maintenance is not carried out. In the slum areas of Lima, many of the large, two storey houses were originally occupied by one single family with the resources to carry out periodic maintenance. Such houses were never intended to be occupied by 20 or 30 different families. Under the circumstances, all

Andrew Maskrey/Juvenal Medina/Predes

Building such as this, originally built for one family, are now multi-occupied, and show evidence of rapid deterioration as maintenance is no longer carried out. If there were an earthquake, the building would be a death trap.

the installations, especially water and drainage, stairways and passages and the structure in general, have deteriorated rapidly.

Lack of maintenance is due primarily to the tenure patterns. Low rents give owners no incentive to maintain or improve their properties. Rent legislation effectively froze rents in older properties; many families pay token sums. Many owners do not bother to collect rent, with the result that they start to lose control over their property. Through inconclusive law suits over inheritance, many properties no longer have a clear legal owner, who could take responsibility for maintenance.

Tenants occupying the building collectively have no clear responsibility for maintaining it and their low incomes prevent them from carrying out repairs, except the most urgent ones, for example to the water supply. There is little social organisation, a further factor which inhibits maintenance. Because of the level of accumulated deterioration, any attempt to restore buildings would now require an enormous investment - beyond the capacities of tenants and owners alike.

Over the years the condition of housing in the critical areas has deteriorated drastically. Every few months, Lima's newspapers report a case of families escaping death as their house suddenly collapsed around them. In the event of a destructive earthquake, thousands of such buildings could collapse, threatening the lives of tens of thousands of families.

Conclusions

Seismic disasters in Lima are not caused simply by earthquakes, which are natural events which have always characterised the Peruvian coast, but also by the vulnerability of people living in overcrowded conditions in dilapidated buildings. The increase in vulnerability of the city has been brought about by a complex process of change in the economy and its urban centres. The location and growth of the city, the rapid industrialisation and massive population movements, the form of buildings and urban spaces, and the ownership of land and houses are all factors affected by that process and together make up an evolving pattern of vulnerability.

The people most vulnerable to the effects of an earthquake in the city are those with very limited options in terms of access to housing and employment. The inhabitants of critical areas would not choose to live there if they had any alternative, nor do they deliberately neglect the maintenance of their overcrowded and deteriorated tenements. For them it is the best-of-the-worst of a number of disaster-prone scenarios such as having nowhere to live, having no way of earning a living and having nothing to eat. Given that these other risks have to be confronted on a daily basis, it is hardly surprising that people give little priority to the risk of destruction by earthquake, which may not occur for another half-century or more.

Low income families in Lima only have freedom to choose between different kinds of disaster. Within the options available, people seek to minimise vulnerability to one kind of hazard even at the cost of increasing their vulnerability to another.

Chapter Three
HUAICOS AND FLOODS IN THE RIMAC VALLEY, PERU
Introduction
Every year between December and April huaicos (a quechua word meaning violent mudslides) and floods occur in Peru's Rimac Valley, affecting:

- human settlements located in the side valleys and on the flood plains of the Rimac, Santa Eulalia and Blanca rivers;
- the railway and highway which connect Lima to the central mountains and jungle and which run parallel to the river;
- farmland and crops through erosion, flooding and alluvion;
- irrigation channels and systems;
- Lima's drinking water supply.

Between 1980 and 1983, 144 huaicos occurred; the impact of huaicos and floods in the regional economy is enormous. When the central highway and railway are blocked or destroyed production losses are huge, as a large proportion of Peru's mineral and agricultural production is carried on these two routes. In 1984, both routes were blocked for a total of 15 days. When the level of solid material entering Lima's reservoir passes a given level water cannot be treated, supply has to be reduced by at least 25% and enormous amounts have to be spent on cleaning the plant. Lima's population suffers from water shortage in the hottest months of the year. There is also loss of human life and destruction of housing. In 1983, 35 people died in huaicos, 96 houses were destroyed and 622 people were left homeless. Losses in 1987 were greater still.

This case study looks at the way the natural hazard arises and how disasters are caused because of the vulnerability of people resulting from changes in the regional economy and its urban centres and settlement patterns.

Geodynamic Activity in the Rimac Valley
The Rimac basin is located on the Pacific coast of Peru. The area of the basin, including its principal tributaries, is 3517 square kilometres, which represents about 0.25% of the total area of Peru. The Rimac's source is at 5000 metres above sea level in the Central Cordillera of the Andes

and the river reaches the Pacific at Callao only 120 kilometres later. It has 39 important tributaries.

As in other valleys on the western slopes of the Peruvian Andes, the Rimac Valley has different ecological zones. The lower valley, up to around 2000 metres above sea level, is sub-tropical desert, with an almost total absence of rain and little or no vegetation except in irrigated areas. Along the coast and for some 20 kilometres inland a humid blanket of low cloud hangs over the valley for six months of the year, from May to November. Above 2000 metres cactus and xerophitic plants appear. Between 2800 and 3800 metres, the valley is semi-arid with a substantial amount of vegetation, especially after the rainy season in April and May. Between 3800 and 4300 metres above sea level, the climate is cold and humid and the landscape characterised by high Andean pasture. Above that level, shattered rock and scree lead up to the snowfields of the Central Cordillera of the Andes. In the lower valley the rainfall rarely exceeds 50 mm a year while in the upper valley it is over 1000 mm, concentrated in the months December to April.

While earthquakes occur periodically, the most common hazards in the area are huaicos and floods. Huaico is a quechua term applied to a form of water erosion which, although particularly characteristic of the Andes, is common to other mountainous areas of the world. A huaico is a fast and violent flow of mud which may also contain stones and rocks of different sizes. Huaicos only occur under particular topographical, climatic, geological and ecological conditions. In the Rimac Valley between 1500 metres and 4000 metres above sea level, conditions are extremely propitious for the formation of huaicos.

A huaico works like a funnel. In the headwaters of the tributary valleys, extremely heavy rains fall over a very short period. Of the rain that falls, one part evaporates, one part infiltrates the soil and one part runs off on the surface. If the ground were covered by trees and vegetation a far greater proportion of the water would infiltrate or evaporate, minimising run off. However, in the Rimac Valley, the run off is very heavy. Vegetation is scarce after the long dry season, leaving the soils exposed to the action of water. Due to centuries of deforestation, overgrazing and inappropriate management of soil and water, man has made conditions even more propitious for erosion. Huaicos are not purely geophysical phenomena; there is a strong human influence in their formation.

Because of the steepness of the slopes, run off is extremely rapid, giving rise to sudden upsurges of water in the valley streams. Given the lack of vegetation and the presence of loose and fractured rock the runoff is highly erosive, causing small landslides and the formation of gullies. By the time the gullies have joined together the runoff is already carrying considerable quantities of earth and rock, which increases its erosive power still more.

The steepness of the gradient and the narrowness of the valleys mean that the huaico descends at great speed towards the valley bottom. Further erosion takes place adding even more soil, rock and vegetation to the water. At the main valley, where the side valleys open out and the gradient lessens, the huaico slows down, depositing mud and rock in a broad cone. Although every huaico is different, two principal kinds can be identified - alluvions, which are composed of large masses of rock and stone; and torrents, which are mainly water and mud. Both kinds of huaico are common in the Rimac valley.

On days of intense rainfall, huaicos descend simultaneously down the side valleys and tributaries of the Rimac, increasing the flow of the river dramatically. In the dry season, the river has a flow of only 10 - 15 cubic metres per second. In the rainy season the flow may increase to as much as 200 - 300 cubic metres per second and the Rimac itself becomes a giant huaico. In the lower valley, the river erodes its banks and spills out on to the floodplain. The river bed fills up with rocks and stones, causing the river to change course and rise in level each year. While it is not possible to predict when huaicos will occur, it is perfectly possible to determine both critical areas and the probabilities of huaicos occurring in those areas. It would also be possible to develop downriver warning systems to give time for evacuation, but these would be expensive to install.

Vulnerability to Huaicos and Floods

While a knowledge of geodynamics is essential to understand why, when and where huaicos and floods occur, it is not sufficient to explain why these hazards cause disasters. To analyse the vulnerability of people, it is equally important to look at their economic activities and settlements.

The Rimac Valley is heavily populated, with Lima and the port of Callao located on the alluvionic cone where the valley fans out at the coast. This case study concentrates on two urban districts, which straddle the river to the east of the city (Lurigancho-Chosica and Chaclacayo) and with the rural province of Huarochiri, beyond.

Although administratively part of metropolitan Lima, Chosica and Chaclacayo are still distinct towns, separated from the city by tracts of farmland. Both were formed in the late 19th century around stations on

Aerial view of Matucana, Rimac Valley, showing the vulnerable location of the main road, railway and buildings in the floodplain. Erosion is clearly visible on the steep sides of the surrounding mountains, particularly where vegetation cover is denuded.

Andrew Maskrey/Juvenal Medina/Predes

the Central Railway to the Sierra and as winter resorts for Lima's upper class. Both still preserve their original urban nucleus situated on high ground away from the river. The population growth of both areas since the 1940s has been through the formation of pueblos jovenes by invasion on marginal land. In both districts pueblos jovenes have occupied floodplain land along the river, steep rocky hillsides and the alluvionic cones of the side valleys. Private housing developments have also been built on the lower alluvionic cones, though most have occupied farm land.

Above Chosica lies the Province of Huarochiri. Huarochiri is rural, with a low population density. In an area of 4200 square kilometres the total population is only 65,000. A third of that population is concentrated in four urban areas: Santa Eulalia and Ricardo Palma (which geographically are part of Chosica) and San Mateo and Matucana (which lie above Chosica in the upper Rimac valley). The population of Huarochiri is static, natural growth being siphoned off through migration to Lima.

The Rimac Valley is the major communication route between Lima and the central Sierra and Selva of Peru. Both the Central Railway and the Central Highway follow the valley from the coast to the pass of Ticlio at 4800 metres above sea level. A large part of Peru's mineral production for export passes along the railway while much of the food Lima consumes is brought along the highway, making both routes of strategic importance. The river generates electricity for Lima, there being no less than four hydroelectric power stations on the rivers Rimac and Santa Eulalia. The river also provides Lima with much of its drinking water, via a reservoir and treatment plant on the eastern outskirts of the city.

Location is the principal factor which conditions vulnerability to huaicos and floods in the Rimac Valley. The forms and structures of buildings are very much secondary factors, especially in the event of alluvionic huaicos which bury or destroy all in their path. In the case of floods, however, adobe buildings are more vulnerable than those of brick and concrete.

Vulnerability is also determined by non-locational factors. In the same location, residents of a high income urbanisation have a far better chance to resist the impact of a disaster and to recover than residents of a low income pueblo joven. In general, the pueblos jovenes and their inhabitants suffer generalised vulnerability, characterised by low and unstable incomes, lack of basic amenities, such as drinking water supply, and poor housing conditions. Vulnerability to hazards such as huaicos and floods is only one aspect of a permanent emergency.

Every year people in some pueblos jovenes lose their belongings or their homes, representing almost the whole of their resources accumulated over many years. Recovery is difficult, or even impossible in some cases. Whereas residents of high income areas can afford substantial investments to protect their settlements from hazards such as floods and rockfalls, residents of pueblos jovenes have no such surplus. The state invests large sums to protect strategic infrastructure such as railways, roads and power stations. Little or nothing is invested in the protection of low income settlements and their inhabitants or to help them recover from disaster.

Different levels of vulnerability can be identified in the valley. The most vulnerable areas are pueblos jovenes and some small towns and villages in Huarochiri which are located directly in the floodplain or aluvionic cones. Those who lose farm land, irrigation infrastructure, water supply and road links are also vulnerable. Better off families with more land and a variety of sources of income are less affected than those with unstable subsistence incomes.

The whole metropolitan area of Lima-Callao and indeed the regional and national economy is vulnerable to huaicos. When the central highway and railway are closed, food increases in price and becomes scarce and mineral exports cease.

Urbanisation in the Rimac Valley

Annual disasters did not always occur in the Rimac valley. In Inca and pre-Inca periods we have no evidence to suggest major destruction of human settlements from huaicos or floods nor can we suppose that geodynamic activity in the area was less intense than it is now.

The ruins of Cajamarquilla in the lower valley show that the area, like other coastal valleys in central and northern Peru, was a major centre for pre-Inca civilisation. The fertile irrigated agricultural land was able to support large urban centres which were located on higher ground in situations where they were not vulnerable to huaicos and floods.

After the Spanish invasion in 1532 new settlements sprung up along the coast. Lima, the capital, was located in the lower Rimac Valley. Unlike the pre-Colombians, the Spanish built towns and roads in the valley bottom.

The main period of urbanisation has been over the last 50 years. Since the 1940s, both Chosica and Chaclacayo have experienced rapid urban expansion. Whereas earlier settlements were located in secure areas the recent urbanisation process has concentrated people and

Andrew Maskrey/Juvenal Medina/Predes

Aerial view of San Mateo, Rimac Valley. The side valley in the centre of the photograph shows how erosion can be controlled if the vegetation cover is maintained and agricultural land is terraced.

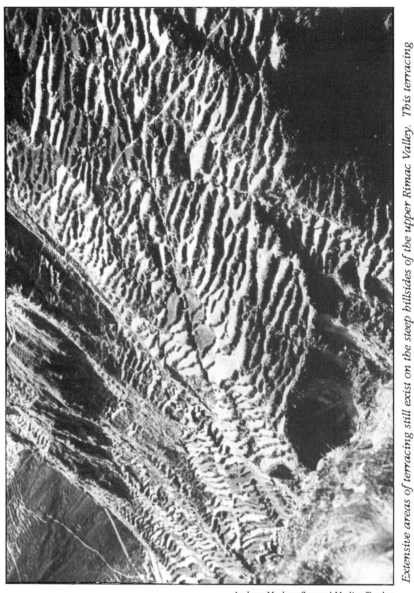

Extensive areas of terracing still exist on the steep hillsides of the upper Rimac Valley. This terracing would once have controlled soil erosion effectively by maximising infiltration and minimising run off.

Andrew Maskrey/Juvenal Medina/Predes

buildings where geodynamic activity is most intense, causing annual disasters to occur. Urbanisation in the Rimac valley has been extensive because of its closeness to Lima and the presence of two main transport routes linking Lima to the interior of the country.

The only land available for low income families has been in vulnerable locations. In both Chosica and Chaclacayo pueblos jovenes were formed on the floodplain of the river Rimac, at the end of side valleys and on the steep valley sides - land of no commercial value. Better quality land in most but not all cases has been used for private housing development. In the alluvionic cones, in the lower valley, large huaicos only occur every 50 years or so and hazard risk was not taken into consideration in people's decision to settle in the area. The same cannot be said of settlements on the floodplain, where floods occur regularly. In reality, the shortage of land to invade and the need to take into account other locational factors, such as closeness to work and availability of transport, means that for most people hazard risk assumes a secondary importance. People face a series of problems. Even though there may be full awareness of the potential damage to be caused by huaicos and floods, everyday problems such as lack of drinking water and insecurity of tenure can assume far greater importance for many poor people.

Increased Erosion

The occurrence of huaicos and floods can be explained by the geological and climatic conditions existing in the valley. But if there is little which can be done to affect either climate or geology, it is possible to manage both soil and water in ways that either accelerate or retard the formation of huaicos. There are a series of measures which can be used to control water erosion:

- **mechanical methods** (the construction of terracing on hillsides, drainage channels, etc.);
- **agronomic measures** (crop rotation, contour planting etc.);
- **agrostological measures** (control of pastures);
- **forestry measures** (conservation and reproduction of trees and forests).

All the evidence suggests that the Incas and their predecessors were expert geotechnicians, managing resources in a way that minimised geodynamic activity. In the upper Rimac valley large areas of terracing still exist on the steep hillsides. Although now abandoned and rapidly deteriorating, this terracing would once have controlled soil erosion effectively, maximising rainwater infiltration and minimising run off. In areas where terracing has been well maintained there is little evidence of erosion, demonstrating that the formation of huaicos can to some extent be controlled. In addition, the small patches of native woodland which dot those slopes which are inaccessible to cattle are only vestiges of the natural forests which centuries ago would have afforded additional protection to the soil in the headwaters of the valleys. Obviously huaicos and floods did occur in pre-Colombian times, but evidently there was not the uncontrolled erosion which is taking place in the valley today.

The control was possible because of the way in which society was organised and resources were used. The extremely sophisticated techniques for managing soil and water - building terraces, filling them with fertile soil brought from the valley bottoms and irrigating them through a complex system of channels - depended on a tight social and territorial organisation.

Under the Incas, the population of Peru was roughly the same size as it is today. Although it is important not to idealise pre-colonial societies, as far as we know everyone was well fed and food reserves were maintained to allow for variations in production through drought or climatic change. Security rather than vulnerability characterised the society.

After the Spanish invasion, this security was systematically destroyed. The indigenous population became a resource to be exploited and was decimated through European disease and ill-treatment, being used as forced labour in the mines and in the large ranches or haciendas, which the colonists set up. Indigenous farmers were driven on to marginal land where subsistence was only just possible. The Spanish were interested not in maintaining a high level of agricultural production but in extracting gold and silver for transshipment to Spain. Existing indigenous crops and farming systems were not respected. Instead, crops, animals and farming practices were brought in which were alien to the Andes and not ecologically suited to the region. Because the social organisation necessary to build and maintain enormous engineering works such as terraces and irrigation systems was destroyed, it is not surprising that since the 16th century these have steadily deteriorated. Once maintenance of the terraces was neglected and cattle and goats started to destroy the vegetation cover, erosion progressively increased.

In the present century, the rural areas in the upper valley have become steadily depopulated through migration to nearby towns or to Lima. The system of subsistence agriculture based on the peasant community and largely outside of the money economy has been replaced by production governed by market forces.

Because of low prices paid for agricultural products, in the interests of the urban market, producers earn barely enough to cover their costs. Peasant farmers are forced to migrate and their land is put to more profitable use. Areas in the Rimac valley formerly used for cultivating potatoes and maize are now grazed by cattle and goats. Meat and dairy production is far more profitable than potato growing and employs fewer people. With the exodus of the population and the change over from subsistence crop production to commercial cattle raising, the remaining vestiges of traditional social organisation have broken down, accelerating the deterioration of terraces and irrigation works.

New employment opportunities in mining, commerce and services also encourage the move away from agriculture. Wages, although low are considerably higher than can be gained through crop growing. Agriculture becomes a secondary or tertiary activity and population shifts from the small villages on high ground to large established towns on communication routes in the valley bottoms. This has been very evident in the Rimac valley. Lima's concentration of industrial and commercial activities has also been a strong catalyst for migration and the change in the employment structure. The availability of alternative employment opportunities and easy accessibility to urban markets has increased migration, destroyed agricultural production and urbanised the population. In Peru it is only in peripheral areas where accessibility to markets is more difficult and other employment opportunities do not exist that traditional agricultural patterns and social organisation persist.

The result of these changes, in the upper Rimac valley, can be summarised in terms of overgrazing, deforestation and the abandonment of terraces and water management. This accelerates erosion which in turn increases geodynamic activity.

Conclusions

The Rimac Valley presents visible symptoms of progressive disaster. The vulnerability of the regional economy and its urban centres is a consequence of socioeconomic, political and territorial changes which began in the 16th century. The modernisation of the urban economy, the destruction of the rural economy, the closeness to Lima, the existence of major communication routes to the interior and what are in any case highly propitious ecological conditions for huaicos and floods, have led to the progressive acceleration of geodynamic activity and the urbanisation of vulnerable locations - creating conditions for repeated disaster. It is equally clear that the specific factors causing vulnerability in the Rimac Valley are in turn influenced by the wider forces of national and international economics and politics.

Huaicos and floods in the Rimac Valley affect predominantly low income families in pueblos jovenes, who have no option but to occupy vulnerable land. Living conditions in general in the pueblos jovenes are in a permanent state of emergency, characterised by lack of drinking water, poor accessibility and inadequate housing. The effects of huaicos and floods are only one aspect of this continuous disaster.

In the Rimac Valley, it is clear that not only do natural hazards affect social and economic structures, but social and economic processes affect ecological conditions, accelerating and magnifying hazards.

The disaster is a downward spiral. Destruction of houses and settlements makes people even more vulnerable. Unable to find new and better locations to live in people are forced back into the same or even more vulnerable conditions.

Vulnerability characterises life in the pueblos jovenes. The periodic occurrence of huaicos and floods only serves to exacerbate the situation, making poor people poorer and creating conditions for new disasters.

Chapter Four
VULNERABILITY IN OTHER CONTEXTS
A Comparative Analysis

The two Peruvian case studies have shown how, in two contexts and faced with different hazards, vulnerability to disaster evolves within historical processes of economic transformation and urbanisation. Although the hazards are different the causes of the vulnerability are remarkably similar. The way in which people assign priority to risk of natural hazard, is complex. From the case studies, it is clear that people's actions are not irrational. When daily survival itself is fragile, people are forced to adopt settlement patterns, housing solutions and economic activities which make them vulnerable to hazards.

Vulnerability to hazard may be chosen as a lesser evil, because the hazard is infrequent, compared to the more pressing day to day problems of homelessness, lack of income or inaccessibility. Poor people are vulnerable to hazard as a result of processes that have deprived them of any power to affect their own physical, social or economic environment. Their only freedom of choice is to choose between different disasters.

These conclusions are not unique to central Peru. Nine documented case studies from other contexts have also been examined. These are not meant to be a conclusive and representative sample but serve to provide additional evidence of the ways in which vulnerability arises and manifests itself.

Case studies on Vulnerability

1. ARGENTINA: El Gran Resistencia, Chaco.
Kind of Hazard - Flood

The vulnerability of the area to floods increased due to two factors:
"The regulatory efficiency of the water-soil-vegetation system of the Chaquena region in the basin of the river Plate has deteriorated rapidly owing to changes in land use and an inadequate management of renewable natural resources. The deforestation in the upper reaches of the basin produced a reduction in the interception of rain water and in the infiltration of rain water in the ground.

"The process of urbanisation of Gran Resistencia has increased over the last few years. Urban growth has overcrowded existing urban areas and occupied floodplain and low lying areas."

Source: CAPUTO, HARDOY, HERZER, 'La Inundacion en el Gran Resistencia (Provincia del Chaco, Argentina) 1982 - 1983', in *Desastres Naturales y Sociedad en America Latina*, Grupo Editora Latinoamericana, Buenos Aires, 1985.

2. BRAZIL: Sertao (North-east)
Kind of Hazard - Drought

"Research carried out since the 1970s shows clearly that the effect of the drought is concentrated selectively in a homogeneous social group: those who do not have access to land and who suffer all the symptoms of rural poverty. This part of the population depends, for its subsistence, on the annual food crops which are most vulnerable to the drought, in contrast to large landowners, whose basic activities are cattle raising and cotton growing.
"The problem of the drought is not just a problem of lack of water. Nor is it just a problem of the ecological and economic adaptation of economic activities. It is fundamentally the problem of the poverty of certain social groups.
"According to the perception of the victims of the drought: the problem could not be reduced to the simple natural and technical dimension of the lack of water and the loss of crops. Among the principal problems mentioned, two thirds refer to a wider and more critical social dimension: poverty, hunger, illness, low salary."

Source: PESSOA, Dirceu, 'Sequias en el Nordeste del Brasil: de la Catastrofe Natural a la Fragilidad Social', in *Desastres Naturales y Sociedad en America Latina*, Grupo Editora Latinoamericana, Buenos Aires, 1985.

3. DOMINICAN REPUBLIC: Monte Plata; Bayaguana; Sabana Grande de Boya.
Kind of Hazard - Cyclone.

Three kinds of specific vulnerability are identified: vulnerability of rural communities to flooding in low-lying areas; erosion and falling crop yields in upland areas; vulnerability of urban shanty settlements on marginal land to hurricanes:

The vulnerability is created by "certain social and economic processes implicit in state and private development of commercial agricultural production at the expense of small scale producers. Such processes include the concentration of land into larger units for the purposes of mechanisation, entailing the dispossession of existing producers either by coercion or by the play of market forces, such as the rise in land prices which (in the context of inflation, rising prices in basic foodstuffs and consumer goods, combined with the small-scale producers' limited access to credit in order to increase their production) encouraged the small producers to sell their land and seek alternative sources of livelihood.

"In the cases presented, the commercialisation of agriculture (in particular the extension of sugar cane production, sensitive to fluctuations in prices in the world commodity market) has not only entailed widespread deforestation of fertile lowlands but has also forced small-scale farmers into marginal areas either to farm patches of land around the sugar cane or to invade the poorer hill areas (leading to over-farming and erosion). At the same time it has also been the cause of migration to the urban areas and the growth of shanty settlements."

Source: JEFFERY, Susan E, 'The Creation of Vulnerability to Natural Disaster: Case Studies from the Dominican Republic', *Disasters* Vol.6 No.1, 1982.

4. ECUADOR: Quito.

Kind of Hazard - Floods, mudslides, landslides, earthquakes.

This case analyses the vulnerability of the inhabitants of peri-urban settlements in Quito. The vulnerability has various dimensions:

"Popular settlements present problems of insecurity and fragility, both in physical terms, with geographically inadequate sites, with gradients often of 60% and easily subject to landslides and in legal terms given that most settlements have not obtained legal recognition.

"The concentration of a deficit of infrastructure, access, transport and services in the popular settlements.

"The location of popular settlements in areas which are prone to floods, landslides and mudslides due to:

- the increase in urban population and its land needs;
- sudden increase in land prices in Quito due to speculation;
- the process of urban renovation in the centre of the city, which pushes low-income residents to the periphery.

"The population of the settlements live in a situation of permanent emergency, which acquires dramatic characteristics when affected by natural hazards.

"The overall deterioration of the real incomes of the peri-urban population due to the economic crisis of the country, at the same time as a rise in food prices because of the loss of harvests and destruction of agricultural zones in rural areas."

Source: GARCIA, Jorge, 'Los Desastres Naturales Afectan a los Mas Pobres', in *Desastres Naturales en America Latina*, Grupo Editora Latinoamericana, 1985.

5. INDIA: Andhra Pradesh.
Kind of Hazard - Cyclone

Differential vulnerability to cyclones in the Krishna Delta area is not so much a function of location as much as of assets and resources:

"Size of family and consequent increase in labour power is closely correlated with an increase in assets and income opportunities.

"Illness plays a major role in the decline of households' economic position, with subsequent forced sale of assets to meet medical costs.

"Small households seem to be particularly vulnerable.

"The vulnerability of a household is determined by the interaction between its resources and assets and external forces acting on them either singly or in combination. The key household characteristics are its size, structure and the age and health of its members. The key assets are those from which income is earned. Household characteristics and their resource and asset position are partly determined biologically but mainly by the income opportunities in the environment. These income opportunities are largely determined by the historical interrelationships between people and their environment and government policies and the environment itself which is subject to the climate and exposure to natural phenomena.

"The relationship between people and their environment and the historical social relations of production were the result of individual and collective decisions made about income opportunities, on the spot, whereas today's land use and resource allocation policy decisions, by their complex nature, are made by people who live outside the area in question.

"It was also of interest to find that perceptions of risk, in terms of the principal threat to livelihood, had changed and were more strongly correlated with socioeconomic status, than with housetype and/or location."

Source: WINCHESTER, Peter, 'Community Vulnerability in a Cyclone Prone Area of South India; Housing Provision and other Government Policies', CIB/W73 Conference, India, 1984.

6. PAKISTAN: Bakulti Village, Yasin.

Kind of Hazard - Floods, mudslides, landslides and earthquakes.

Vulnerability was summarised as a combination of the following factors:

"1. A lack of surplus produce for trade and a lack of cash capital for entrepreneurial activity.

"2. Increasing pressure on land resulting in less produce per hectare. This mainly results from abandoning the traditional practice of leaving fields fallow for between one and three years. The potential for serious food shortages is considerable and in addition, there have been recent severe government restrictions on hunting activities, previously a valuable protein source ...

"3. A lack of adequate communication, especially of vehicles and roads to facilitate marketing of any surplus.

"4. A lack of employment opportunities. Road construction work is seasonal, in the summer, which is precisely the time of heaviest agricultural commitment.

"5. Increasing use of land which is subject to flooding.

"6. Little real opportunity to cultivate virgin land, mainly because it is not available; irrigation is an extremely tricky process and it is simply not cost effective to construct channels on unstable slopes where they will be destroyed by even a minor landslip.

"7. In the longer term, extensive logging of the hills, which in turn makes them more unstable and thus vulnerable to land slip, and a concomitant shortage of wood plus a lack of cash to buy kerosene for fuel.

"The ability to respond to vulnerability depends largely on the availability of surplus economic resources....The poorest of the poor very often don't survive in the community and become migrants to urban areas, part of the squatter population living in the slums of larger towns.

"The location of the poorer members of the community along the margins of the rivers is additional evidence for the notion that obtaining a livelihood today is more important than some possible future danger that may or may not happen; precautions are only taken for those hazards within the economic means of those under threat, all other fears are suppressed in order that day to day existence can continue."

Source: D'SOUZA, Francia, 'The Socio-Economic Cost of Planning for Hazards - An Analysis of Barkulti Village, Yasin, Northern Pakistan', *International Karakorum Project*, Cambridge University Press, 1984. MOUGHTIN, C, 'Barkulti in the Yasin Valley: A Study of Traditional Settlement Form as a Response to Environmental Hazard', *International Karakorum Project*, Cambridge University Press, 1984.

7. PERU: Cusco.
Kind of Hazard - Drought

This case analyses the severe drought which affected peasant communities in Peru's altiplano in 1983. The vulnerability of the communities to the drought was due to three principal factors:

"1. The amount of cultivated land per person, shows crudely the extreme shortage of land in the southern Andean region.
"2. The gradual process of exhaustion of agricultural activity over the last two decades due to growing indices of overgrazing.
"3. The Agrarian Reform of the 1970s did not manage to transform the structure of land ownership. Rather than redistributing, it concentrated land in an associative form."

Source: LOVON Z. Gerardo, 'El Sur Andino Peruano la Coyuntura de Sequia: 1982 - 1983', in *Desastres y Sociedad en America Latina*, Grupo Editora Latinoamericana, Buenos Aires, 1985.

8. PERU: *Piura*
Kind of Hazard - Flood

The extraordinary rains of 1983 produced extensive flooding which affected agricultural land and production; infrastructure (irrigation; roads; water supply); rural and urban settlements and food supply. The vulnerability of the area is a product of:

"The transformation of an economy of small-scale farmers, with a distribution of land and water and a form of production well suited to the economy of the zone and which persisted until the end of the 19th century, by an economy of large plantations producing cotton for export.

"The disappropriation of land began in the beginning of the present century, when the demand for cotton on the world market generated by the textile industry, attracted foreign capital to the area. Local land owners built new irrigations, forced peasants off the land and used new technology to transform the Piura Valley. The smallholder became a permanent or seasonal worker dependent on a salary. The new structure of land ownership broke the relationship between the local population and the natural resources, which no longer belonged to them (not only land; also forest, pastures, water and villages).

"The introduction of the plantations coincided with a rapid demographic increase. Both smallholdings and settlements were forced out of fertile areas to the limits of the desert. For the smallholders this meant poverty, social disintegration, precarious living conditions and the destruction of a productive system well adapted to the ecological conditions of the area.

"The Agrarian Reform of 1970 changed the ownership of the plantations, returning it to the peasants. However, the productive system remained the same: people depended on a salary and their living conditions didn't improve."

On the contrary, before the plantations:

"A first and superficial investigation, then, discovers in the culture of the zone a rich relation with rivers and floods, which couldn't be any different when life in the region always depended on them."

Source: FRANCO, Eduardo, 'El Desastre Natural en Piura', in *Desastres y Sociedad en America Latina*, Grupo Editora Latinoamericana, Buenos Aires, 1985.

9. TURKEY: Gediz.
Kind of hazard - Earthquake

The way communities cope with vulnerability is not a simple 'learning from experience' process but a complicated series of adjustments to change. Where there are many forms of vulnerability and the resources to avoid them are limited, optimisation of these resources in relation to the local and household priorities become the key measure. This process is an intuitive and experimental one and arrives at certain solutions over a long period of time.

"[These few examples]... outline the delicate balance that the local communities have to maintain for economic, physical and cultural survival at the cost of increasing one type of vulnerability for the sake of avoiding the others. One can say that some of these problems could be solved if there was a better understanding of safe building, or if the local materials and techniques could be improved. However, improvement for the communities with limited economies and resources was a matter of choice, each time optimising these resources according to their priorities."

Source: AYSAN, Yasemin, 'Community Vulnerability in Rural Areas; Gediz; Turkey', CIB/W 73 Conference, India, 1984.

The Evolution of Vulnerability

Specific characteristics of vulnerability evidently vary from area to area and context to context. The cases, however, show up a number of recurring elements.

In rural areas these include unequal access to land, inability to produce a surplus, absence of other income earning opportunities, no access to credit, forced migration to urban areas, ecological damage caused by excessive pressure on natural resources and shortage of materials for housing.

These characteristics have emerged historically through the transformation of local, regional, national and international economies through mechanisms such as unequal distribution of land between social groups (2. Brazil, 5. India, 8. Peru); disappropriation of agricultural land from small farmers by national and foreign capital (2. Brazil, 3. Dominican Republic, 8. Peru); displacement of subsistence production by cash crops or cattle raising for external markets (2. Brazil, 3. Dominican Republic, 8. Peru); introduction of new technologies and crops (8. Peru) and the failure of agrarian reforms to affect the land ownership (7. Peru and 8. Peru).

In urban settlements, the elements include the siting of low income settlements in vulnerable locations (3.Dominican Republic and 4. Ecuador); income levels which barely cover subsistence, deficiencies in services, infrastructure, and transport in low income peri-urban settlements, lack of access to income earning opportunities (4. Ecuador); poor housing conditions and deterioration of existing housing in old inner city areas (4. Ecuador and 9. Turkey).

Urban settlements have also been affected by population increases through natural growth and rural migration (3. Dominican Republic and 4. Ecuador); land speculation and urban renewal in inner city areas (4. Ecuador) and rebuilding following major disasters (9. Turkey).

The evidence from the two Peruvian cases together with the other case-studies shows that vulnerability is a consequence of particular socio-economic processes and structures rather than being characteristic of hazards. Vulnerability to any kind of hazard is essentially determined by poverty.

The effects of the natural hazards and the ecological and economic maladaptation of activities, settlements and building types were also evident in the cases analysed. However, rather than being causes in themselves, they were manifestations and characteristics of patterns of social and economic inequalities. In most cases, people were living in a state of permanent disaster anyway, even without natural hazard. The concentration of economic power in a dominant minority; the introduction of centralising technologies which disappropriate resources from the majority and the subsequent social, economic, political and territorial marginalisation of this majority are the mechanisms through which vulnerability emerges. These mechanisms are characteristics of an international process of the accumulation and concentration of wealth and power.

This process involves a global division of labour and a resulting evolution of vulnerability at the social and territorial periphery of the world economic system. Vulnerability at the social and economic centres of power has been virtually eliminated by being exported to the periphery. Underdevelopment is not a stage on the way to development but an inevitable consequence of development. The more the centre overdevelops, the more the periphery underdevelops and becomes vulnerable.

There is, however, an integral contradiction and instability built in to the current world economic order. The increasing incidence of disasters and the destruction of the ecosphere consequent upon overdevelopment and the exploitation of natural resources menace the stability of the system. Extending the limits of exploitation of marginal groups and of the environment and thereby increasing vulnerability may be essential to continued accumulation of wealth and power and the overcoming of successive crises, in the short term. However the development of self-generated and self-perpetuated crises in different modes of production may eventually lead to their renovation. Vulnerability as itself a cause of the crisis will eventually create conditions for change and transformation.

Response to Vulnerability

In some traditional societies, where the social organisation guaranteed a fairly equitable access to resources, people, their activities and their environment were in a good ecological balance. Societies and communities were able to adjust and adapt to hazards within the limits imposed by knowledge, resource availability and technology. But in other traditional societies life was far from secure. Profound social inequalities existed, leading to the marginalisation of certain groups who then become vulnerable to different hazards. As traditional societies became incorporated or coerced into market economies and increasingly subject to external pressures and constraints which they could not control, vulnerability increased, while the availability of resources and the possibility of avoiding hazards decreased. People cannot adjust or adapt to hazards because they no longer control access to resources, production, exchange and distribution mechanisms. These are controlled by market forces, governments or other external agents. Daily life becomes vulnerable and fragile for many social groups.

Vulnerability can best be understood as a relationship between the forms, means and relations of production. Attention focused on specific, usually physical, aspects of vulnerability is leading research further and further away from a real understanding of why people suffer disaster. If continued research on hazards and their effects on specific forms is to be useful, it must form part of a wider historical analysis on the evolving relationships between people and the forms, means and relationships of production.

People's Perception of Vulnerability

The actions and decisions of people and communities show that they always try to minimise vulnerability when faced with a range of hazards - an attitude which has been referred to as survival strategy. The poorer people become, the more their vulnerability to a variety of hazards increases, and it becomes more difficult to play off one against another to achieve security. People have to balance extremely limited resources to deal with threats like homelessness, landlessness, illness, unemployment, persecution and so on. Faced with such permanent threats people may give little priority to occasional natural hazards. The less frequent and intense the hazard, the less importance is attached to it. Floods which occur every year are more important than an earthquake which occurs once a century. In general, people are unlikely to change or adapt their living patterns and activities to reduce their vulnerability to natural hazard, if it increases their vulnerability to other more pressing threats.

Response to hazard is complicated because destructive natural hazards often compound other kinds of vulnerability. People who have no choice but to live in highly vulnerable settlements and who lose their homes due to flood and earthquake find an already bad housing situation made worse and may face severe difficulties in rehousing themselves. People are often forced in to even more vulnerable locations.

The most important conclusion is that people themselves do not perceive vulnerability as characteristic of natural hazard or limited to the specific time period when hazards strike. People often perceive natural hazards as perfectly ordinary characteristics of the areas where they live. For most people, the separation of 'natural' disaster from the permanent disaster in which they live is not common sense. It is that permanent disaster which explains the impact of natural hazards and not vice versa.

Reducing Vulnerability

If the analysis of vulnerability given above is accepted, it follow that reducing vulnerability is a complex and far-reaching process. Action is necessary at different levels - individual, local, national and international. If the origins and causes of vulnerability lie in social and economic and political forces beyond people's control, then any attempt at reducing vulnerability must involve empowering people, if it is to be truly effective. In the second part of the book, different approaches to reducing vulnerability will be considered in the light of the analysis in the first part of the book.

Building river defences using wire mesh, Rimac Valley.

Andrew Maskrey/Juvenal Medina/Predes

PART TWO

DISASTER MITIGATION

Chapter Five

APPROACHES TO MITIGATION

What is Mitigation?

Mitigation refers to measures which can be taken to minimise the destructive and disruptive effects of hazards and thus lessen the magnitude of a disaster. Mitigation measures can be of different kinds, ranging from physical measures such as flood defences or safe building design to legislation, training and public awareness. Mitigation is an activity which can take place at any time: before a disaster occurs, during an emergency, or after disaster, during recovery or reconstruction.

Since the 1970s, there has been a growing interest in disaster mitigation programmes from governments, international relief agencies and NGOs. There is a large body of literature which argues the case for mitigation and for agencies as well as governments to reallocate at least part of their budgets from relief to mitigation. It is generally recognised, however, that mitigation still has a very low priority on their agenda.

Critique of Mitigation

There is, however, growing criticism of mitigation programmes. Most of these have been top down in approach, managed by large centralised agencies, without any real participation in decision-making by those affected by disaster. They have tended to be large-scale, high technology solutions, reinforcing the conditions of underdevelopment and increasing the sense of helplessness of those affected by the disaster. The emphasis has been on physical measures to address the immediate threat of a natural hazard and not on social changes to address the problems and build up the resources of vulnerable groups of people. As Ian Davis pointed out:

"Many programmes treat the symptom and not the cause. The symptom may be unsafe buildings or vulnerable cropping patterns, but the causes may include all or some of the following: underdevelopment and poverty; control of land by absentee landlords; corruption; lack of education; ....risk reduction policies must rely on both technical measures and on political intervention"(Davis, 1984).

It is argued that top down mitigation:
- only deals with mitigating the risks of specific hazards and not with

reducing vulnerability. As such, it attacks only the symptoms of disaster and not the underlying causes.

- does not take into account the real needs and demands of those affected by disaster. Because they ignore the complexity of most disasters, mitigation measures are frequently irrelevant or even counterproductive in many local situations and programmes rarely achieve their goals.

- is political and generally favours the rich and powerful at the expense of the most vulnerable. Risks are mitigated to avoid political unrest or economic loss and not to reduce the vulnerability of the poor. Some programmes actually reinforce the underlying causes of vulnerability.

An Alternative Approach to Mitigation

As an alternative it is proposed that instead of dealing only with the effects of hazards, mitigation must also address the underlying causes of vulnerability. In addition to physical measures such as reinforcing buildings or raising dykes, mitigation must become a developmental activity which focuses on factors such as land ownership, wealth distribution, rapid urbanisation, and the destruction of natural resources and seeks to address the real causes of poverty and underdevelopment.

However, while an alternative mitigation theory has now been elaborated, there has been little or no attempt to convert this into a coherent mitigation practice. It has proved notoriously difficult to persuade governments to change their development policies, especially when their support comes from a wealthy, powerful and conservative minority. At the same time, CBOs and NGOs working in the field have little real influence over the structural causes of disaster. A vacuum has built up between the theory and practice of mitigation which inhibits action.

This book argues that only when mitigation as an activity is controlled by people and their own autonomous organisations will the mitigation of specific hazards become a vehicle for affecting the underlying causes of vulnerability. The evidence from a number of case studies demonstrates the existence of an alternative mitigation practice, called community based mitigation. These experiences in turn suggest an alternative model and methodology for mitigation, which bridges the existing gap between theory and practice.

Chapter Six
LIMA'S SEISMIC PROTECTION PLAN
Introduction
Lima's Seismic Protection Plan was prepared in 1982 by the Instituto Nacional de Desarollo Urbano (INADUR) for Peruvian Civil Defence. The objective of the Seismic Protection Plan was to formulate technical and legal measures, in the housing sector, to protect Lima and its inhabitants from future earthquakes. The plan was based on a comprehensive study of seismic vulnerability in Lima (see Chapter Two). Even though it was never implemented, the plan and its proposals are well worth examining for two reasons:

- it is a good example of the alternative approach to mitigation, where vulnerability reduction is seen as part of a wider development strategy. Also it is one of very few attempts to carry out pre-disaster planning in a large metropolis like Lima.

- it shows the inevitable limitations of this approach when government is unable to act on the recommendations made.

Approaches to Earthquake Mitigation
Many countries have made important efforts to develop seismology. In Latin America, CERESIS (Centro Regional de Sismologia) coordinates efforts in this direction. By increasing knowledge about earthquakes, it is hoped to reach greater precision in earthquake prediction. Knowing the time and place of seismic events, human and material damage could be minimised, by evacuating people to pre-determined refuges, for example. Unfortunately, in Lima, the benefits of seismology cannot be realised. It is still not possible to achieve a reasonable level of accuracy in prediction. Furthermore, a prediction is only useful if the population is organised, disciplined and prepared to act; otherwise, a prediction produces chaos and panic. In the vulnerable areas of Lima there is little social organisation. The problem is not simply lack of training in civil defence or in evacuation. Training in disaster preparedness would only make sense and have positive results in the context of a genuine and long term process of social organisation of the population.

Seismology provides base data for seismogeological zoning. This combines data on earthquakes with local conditions of soil and geology. It allows the determination of zones where different seismic intensities occur, which can be a useful input to mitigation measures such as land use planning and building regulations. Urban development can be oriented towards low intensity areas, leaving high intensity areas for parks and other low risk uses. Building regulations can be adjusted to the intensities which are expected in each area.

In Lima, such measures would have little impact. Urban development is not directed by land use planning so much as the voracity of urban property capital. Low income groups are forced to occupy marginal land irrespective of seismic intensities, because no other land is available through market mechanisms. Similarly, building regulations are not enforceable for the most part. Even if builders were trained in seismic design criteria, there are other severe constraints. In the slum areas of Lima, tenants and owners have neither the economic capacity nor the will to reinforce or rebuild to adequate technical norms.

Seismic engineers in Peru and elsewhere, have designed new seismic resistant construction systems, materials and structures and to a lesser extent found ways and means of reinforcing existing unsafe buildings. However, this research has not been put into practice. The approach fails to recognise that the way a building is used and transformed over time is usually far more important than the way it is built in the first place. It would be pointless to carry out a widespread renovation of tenements in the slum areas of Lima, without tackling factors such as tenure patterns and rent legislation, which determine the overuse and lack of maintenance of buildings.

In conclusion, neither public education, training, new building regulations or physical mitigation measures would produce the desired improvements in Lima. In the existing political and socioeconomic context, seismology, seismogeological zoning and seismic engineering cannot be properly applied because they tackle only the symptoms of the problem, not the underlying causes, ignoring the real forces which shape the city and the lives of its inhabitants. People put up with poor physical conditions in overcrowded and deteriorated tenement blocks with high earthquake risk, because of the low rents and good access to employment, and because of the lack of other housing. To force people to move to peripheral locations in order to mitigate earthquake risk, or to greatly increase their rents to pay for the rehabilitation of their tenements, would expose them to a permanent social and economic disaster, worse than the seismic disaster from which they might escape.

An Alternative Strategy

An alternative mitigation strategy was designed based on vulnerability reduction - attacking causes not symptoms. Hazard mitigation measures would only play a useful role if they were incorporated within a much broader task of modifying social and economic processes.

The strategy incorporated measures at different levels:

- **the macro-policy level**
- **the urban planning level**
- **the programme and operational level.**

The Macro-Policy Level

Vulnerability and earthquake risk in the critical areas is a consequence of the urbanisation process. Any measures implemented at the local or metropolitan level have only a limited impact unless the direction of the urbanisation process is modified and changed. As urbanisation reflects wider social and economic process, changes depend to a large extent on economic policy. But this is not entirely within the control of national governments in the sense that they may be under severe constraints from international economic forces. However well-intentioned, Third World governments have little capacity to act in favour of their poor when their resources are sucked away in debt repayments, and their exchequers impoverished by falling commodity prices, controlled by international speculative markets.

Reducing vulnerability means acting on factors such as rural-urban migration; the inability of the urban economy to provide subsistence incomes for a substantial percentage of the population; the control of national industry by foreign capital; the burden of servicing the foreign debt and the evolution of the national economy in the context of international markets. Vulnerability reduction at this level would necessitate a radical economic restructuring, with profound social, political and territorial implications. It would require fundamental changes in the world economic order.

The Urban Planning Level

The form of urbanisation in Lima and particularly the concentration of slums in critical areas of the city reflects to a large extent the mechanisms by which land is distributed and used.

To reduce vulnerability urban planning must guarantee a just access to land, infrastructure, services and finance to all who live in the city. This is a political option, challenging powerful and vociferous interest groups and exercising public control over scarce resources, such as land

and housing finance.
Some of the specific recommendations elaborated in the plan were:
1. Decentralising services and economic activities away from the critical areas, thus discouraging a further increase in density. Changing bus routes and moving transport terminals and markets to less congested peripheral areas could influence people's decisions about where to live, taking pressure off the critical areas.
2. Guaranteeing the availability of appropriately located and serviced land for low income families, thus increasing the population turnover in slum areas and avoiding an increase in density and deterioration of both critical areas and of other areas of the city. Accessibility to opportunities for earning a living, and the feasibility of installing services would be key factors in the selection of sites.
3. Creating financial mechanisms to stimulate the use of vacant or unproductive land in central and critical areas for the construction of multifamily housing for rent to low income groups. This would take the pressure off existing housing in the critical areas, avoiding further overcrowding and deterioration.
4. Creating new forms of housing tenure to enable tenants to take over the management and maintenance of their houses, thus preventing deterioration, while avoiding the imposition of high rents.

Programme and Operational Level

At the programme and operations level the following recommendations were made:
1. Reinforcing and repairing existing tenements to provide adequate living conditions for residents and seismic security. These operations would depend on new mechanisms for obtaining land, finance and appropriate tenure as mentioned above.
2. Building new multifamily houses on vacant inner city land for occupants of tenements whose repair would be unrealistic and which would therefore have to be demolished.
3. Preparing for disaster: training for evacuation; precautions within the home; establishing internal and external secure areas and escape routes; removing obstacles and dangers from public and semi-public space; defining the roles of public institutions and emergency services.

Limitations of the Plan

The plan was designed to overcome the deficiencies of conventional approaches to mitigation by addressing the evolution of vulnerability, rather than one of the effects of that vulnerability. The focus of analysis moved from mitigating specific risks towards attacking the underlying conditions of vulnerability. If the plan had been implemented, low income groups in Lima would have become increasingly less vulnerable and the risk of disaster would have been substantially reduced.

However, despite a coherent analysis and set of proposals, the plan was utopian in character and proved to be impossible to implement. It was formulated within a government agency and contained technical and legal instrumentation for government action. Its implementation presupposed that the government politically represented the interests of disadvantaged and vulnerable groups such as the residents of the critical areas and had the necessary control and authority over powerful interest groups to carry out social, economic and political changes in favour of the disadvantaged and vulnerable.

At the time, central and local government had neither the resources, the authority nor the political will to carry out sweeping recommendations of this kind.

Earthquake Preparedness and Mitigation - the Community Based Alternative

The limitations refer to the strategy to implement the plan and not to the coherence of its proposals. To reject the proposals would be to reject the possibility of a historical transformation of vulnerable conditions. Such a transformation is possible, but its motive force is more likely to be low income groups actually at risk rather than government. The strategy of low income groups would obviously be very different. Instead of global economic change and urban reform setting the scene for specific risk mitigation measures, the implementation of specific risk mitigation measures would act as the political lever for achieving medium and long term reform. A viable community based alternative might have the following stages:

1. Motivating organisation at the community level around specific existing social needs (which almost certainly do not include mitigation).

2. Building up awareness and consciousness of earthquake risk through the implementation of disaster preparedness measures. These measures could be carried out by community based organisations (CBOs) without requiring resources or substantial changes in government policy and would serve to reinforce local organisation.

3. Formulating specific risk mitigation proposals such as reinforcing, rehabilitating and rebuilding tenements. The implementation of the proposals, through a number of pilot projects, would require the exertion of political pressure to obtain expropriation of land, the

creation of appropriate financial mechanisms and tenure arrangements, from central and local government.

Bringing about urban reform and significant economic change in order to reduce vulnerability, is a long term task, and would depend on a much wider level of political activity at the metropolitan and national levels.

The community based alternative would use mitigation at the local level to reinforce organisation, build up political consciousness and reduce long term vulnerability at the metropolitan and national levels. It would attack the causes and not just the symptoms of the problem, but do so through a strategy for immediate action.

Seismological predictions and techniques such as seismic engineering acquire a completely different meaning in community based mitigation. By increasing people's understanding of the physical factors affecting vulnerability they can become a vehicle for building up the political consciousness necessary to motivate and direct action to reduce vulnerability.

The only way to test the validity of the community based approach proposed here would be through the implementation of a pilot programme, by a local non-governmental organisation (NGO). So far neither government agencies, CBOs nor NGOs have been involved in this kind of mitigation programme in the critical areas of Lima.

Chapter Seven
RIMAC VALLEY PROJECT
Introduction
Between 1983 and 1985, PREDES, an NGO founded by three members of the INADUR team, implemented a project to explore the potential of community based mitigation under real field conditions. The Rimac Valley was chosen for the project because:

- disasters due to floods, huaicos and landslides occur almost every year, with a serious effect on both local people and the regional economy;
- the right to physical security is a generalised demand of the CBOs of the area;
- the valley contains a variety of different settlement patterns, hazard types and CBOs but at the same time is geographically compact and accessible from Lima;
- no other NGO was working with the CBOs of the area.

The hypothesis of PIEVAR (Proyecto, Integral, Experimental de Asistencia Tecnica, Estudio y Capacitacion en el Valle Rimac) was that through taking over responsibility for mitigation, CBOs could move beyond the specific context of disaster to bring about the wider policy changes necessary to reduce vulnerability. Disaster mitigation could become an opportunity for CBOs to deepen their consciousness and strengthen their organisation. They could innovate or rescue mitigation techniques which, because they are socially and culturally appropriate do not create dependency or subordination. As a result of their increased strength and self-confidence they would then be able to begin to influence government policy and legislation

PREDES formed a team of professionals from different disciplines, who acted as independent advisors to the CBOs of the area. The team worked with people and their organisations in three different but complementary ways.:

- **through popular education**, creating opportunities for CBOs to reflect on the disaster problem they faced and through increasing consciousness become more effective;
- **through technical assistance**, providing a specialised technical an

socioeconomic advisory service to CBOs, for the design, implementation and management of mitigation projects;
- **through research and planning**, studying both hazards and the vulnerability of the area in order to develop policy alternatives and plans for hazard mitigation and vulnerability reduction.

PIEVAR was a pilot project, developed within an action/research framework in order to generate methodologies and technologies which could be useful to other NGOs working in other areas. As an example of mitigation practice, it provides important elements for the design of a community based mitigation methodology.

The Disasters of 1983 and 1984

PIEVAR began in the context of a series of disastrous huaicos which occurred in the area in 1983, after unusually heavy rains caused by the effects of El Nino current. In both the upper and lower valley extensive damage was caused, with large numbers of houses being destroyed.

Andrew Maskrey/Juvenal Medina/Predes

All that was left of a home after the disastrous flood in February 1984, in Chaclacayo, Rimac Valley.

In February 1984, the principal disasters were in the lower valley and caused by floods rather than huaicos. The worst affected were smallholders, who farmed marginal land on the river banks. The floods also affected pueblos jovenes in Chaclacayo.

Different kinds of disaster are a daily reality for low income people in the Rimac Valley. The struggle for subsistence, the lack of drinking water, as well as transport and housing problems are everyday problems for the majority in the area. But people do not remain passive when their homes and livelihoods are affected by huaicos and floods; their mitigation actions are mainly articulated through their own settlement organisations or CBOs.

Community based organisations in the Rimac Valley

In the upper Rimac Valley, above Chosica, as in other rural areas of Peru, people are organised in Comunidades Campesinas or peasant communities. The community is the legal owner of the land which it allocates amongst its members. It is also responsible for the maintenance of communal infrastructure such as irrigation channels and forests and for managing and implementing improvements. The community is legally recognised and has governing committees which are elected periodically in assemblies. Apart from the community, other sectorial CBOs exist such as irrigation committees and agricultural cooperatives. The Rimac communities tend to be weak and ineffective, at least compared to those in other rural areas where agriculture is still a primary activity. Nonetheless, they remain the most important autonomous community organisations in the area.

Local and central government in the area consists of the Municipality at both District and Provincial level, responsible for local administration and elected every three years and the Governor at District level and the Sub-Prefect at Provincial level, who represent the state and are appointed by the government in power.

In the lower valley, low income people come together through pueblo joven organisations. Different kinds of CBO exist in pueblos jovenes, depending on when settlements were formed. In some pueblos jovenes there are Asociaciones de Pobladores (residents associations), which was the form of organisation most commonly formed until 1970. The association usually has different committees with different functions which are elected in general assemblies.

In other pueblos jovenes, people organise block by block in Comites Vecinales (neighbourhood committees), a form of organisation promoted by the Velasco government in the 1970s. The different neighbourhood committees elect a central committee, which is responsible for promoting the development of the pueblo joven as a whole. Unlike Comunidades Campesinas, pueblo joven organisations have no judicial status, nor do they hold land titles. However, they have de facto responsibility for negotiating with central and local government for land, for the installation of services and other improvements. Other CBOs also exist in pueblo jovenes; Mothers Clubs, Community Kitchens, Glass of Milk Committees and so on. In some pueblo jovenes these organisations achieve greater profile, importance and legitimacy than the settlement organisation itself, a change which has been apparent in Lima as a whole during the 1980s. In the lower valley, organisations have attempted to coordinate and federate. In Chaclacayo, the Federation of Popular Settlements groups together both pueblos jovenes and other low income settlements in the District, while the Multisectoral Committee for River Defence groups settlements on the floodplain. In Chosica, similarly there is the United Committee of the Left Bank and the Committee for the Improvement of the Northern Cone. As in the upper valley, the Municipalities of Chosica and Chaclacayo were important bases of support for the CBOs.

Response to Disaster

People's response to disaster depends on the specific contexts in which floods and huaicos occur. In areas of the valley where these hazards occur only occasionally, there is little or no preventive action. People organise to respond to disaster only after it occurs, and once the emergency period passes mitigation loses importance. In contrast, in areas where disaster occurs annually, mitigation actions are continuous and may be the single highest priority for the CBO.

The principal mitigation measure which CBOs carry out is the construction of flood defences, usually concrete defence walls. These defences are normally planned and implemented by the CBO itself. Families provide labour as well as quotas for materials. CBOs also negotiate with government agencies for materials, technical assistance and also for support through food-for-work programmes. Walls are built both before and after emergency periods. After disaster, affected communities may seek relocation in safe areas, demanding land and temporary housing from central and local government. Usually, this meets with little success and people are forced to remain indefinitely in temporary refuge areas, or else return to their original location, exposing themselves to the risk of new disaster.

The state also has its own mitigation strategy in the area. Government agencies and utility companies invest enormous sums in the protection of important infrastructure, with an increasing tendency to invest in the pre-disaster phase and not just in reconstruction. As an example, both the central highway and the central railway have been rerouted to avoid the most vulnerable areas of the valley and the consequent need to spend huge annual amounts in repairs.

In contrast, few government resources are put into protecting pueblo jovenes, and any measures taken are inadequate and badly planned. Protective works are usually undertaken only after pressure from CBOs and public opinion, in response to emergency situations, when it is difficult for the work to be carried out effectively.

The Civil Defence system and the Red Cross provides food, medical supplies and tents as well as prefabricated emergency housing to those who suffer the effects of huaicos and floods. However, relief is improvised, little training in disaster preparedness is given, nor plans drawn up for evacuations or refuge areas. Once the emergency is over help is withdrawn. Alternative sites for rebuilding are rarely made available. Investments in prefabricated emergency housing are often greater than those which would have been required to provide a permanent, serviced plot in the first place.

A Chronology of the Project

The project was initiated after the 1983 disaster, when PREDES signed an agreement with a committee formed by the CBOs of settlements affected by the disaster, and the Municipality of Chosica. It was agreed that PREDES would evaluate the situation in all the affected areas and provide technical assistance to the committee. In the following months, technical assistance was given to rebuild river defences in two settlements and for planning the relocation of some families who had lost their houses and were living in temporary refuges. None of the relocation projects which were drawn up for the CBOs could be implemented, because people were unable to obtain public land and could not afford to buy. However, the defence projects enabled CBOs in Santa Eulalia to attract investment from a government agency to carry out a number of defence works in the area - the first concrete results of PIEVAR.

Training courses were given to complement and extend specific technical assistance, and to enable CBOs to become more self-reliant in the face of future disasters. The training modules, many of which were produced as manuals and audiovisuals, covered the following areas:

- **human rights and basic needs**
- **community organisation**
- **safe locations for housing**
- **what are natural disasters?**
- **recommendations for protecting houses from floods**
- **recommendations for protecting settlements from floods**
- **government agencies which provide disaster assistance and their legal obligations.**

In the first quarter of 1984, as a result of the February floods, the project extended to the pueblos jovenes and agricultural communities in the lower valley and to the town of Tornamesa in the upper valley. Technical assistance was given to CBOs either to build emergency river defences or to relocate families who had lost their homes. The results of the interventions reinforced the conclusions of the previous year. The local self-help defences which CBOs built with their own resources, offered little long term security, while relocation was impossible as no land was available for low income groups. While technical assistance enabled CBOs to improve the design and resistance of their defences, these in no way represented a permanent solution to the disaster problem in the area.

In February 1984, a forum was held in Chosica organised jointly by Municipalities of the Rimac Valley and supported by two NGOs: PREDES and CIED (Centro de Investigacion, Educacion y Desarollo). Professionals from government agencies, NGOs and universities who had carried out research in the Rimac Valley presented their work and proposed alternative solutions to the disaster problem. Representatives of all the CBOs also participated. The proceedings and conclusions were published in a small book. The Forum was important in a number of ways:

- it outlined strategies for reducing vulnerability in the valley;
- it established relations between PREDES and other professionals and institutions with interest in the disaster problem in the valley;
- it involved the Municipalities in the discussion of the problem;
- it multiplied contacts between CBOs who were able to discuss different solutions to their own particular problems.

River defences built by local community based organisations in the Rimac Valley. PREDES helped with technical assistance and advice in drawing up plans and implementing them.

Hugh Belshaw/Oxfam

A workshop for community leaders, organised by PREDES in 1985. Some of the topics of the workshops were internal organisation, relationships between leaders and community groups and the interaction between community groups and government.

Andrew Maskrey/Juvenal Medina/Predes

The Forum highlighted the growing vulnerability of the area and the close relationship which existed between deforestation, overgrazing and soil erosion in the upper valley and accelerated urbanisation in the lower valley and the occurrence of disasters. It demonstrated the need to complement the local self-help river defences built by individual settlements with comprehensive flood control measures for the river as a whole. It also emphasised that avoiding the formation of huaicos, through the implementation of forestal, mechanical, agronomic and agrostological measures in the upper valley, would be the best way to avoid disaster in the lower valley. In the second quarter of 1984, PREDES carried out six Risk Studies of areas in the upper valley which, using a new approach which integrated geological, ecological and anthropic factors, determined a range of mitigation measures to control the formation of huaicos. The studies were coordinated with the CBOs and Municipalities in each area through meetings and assemblies. Another study was started to devise alternative measures for flood control in the River Rimac itself.

The studies stimulated community organisation in the area. The implementation of the measures proposed required a new level of coordination between CBOs themselves and between CBOs and Municipalities in order to negotiate with central government agencies for resources and machinery. The second half of 1984 saw CBOs from the area coming together to form a Frente de Defensa del Rio Rimac (United Front for the Defence of the River Rimac), which attempted to negotiate a package of defence measures which covered the whole length of the river. While some CBOs were able to implement huaico control measures using local resources and community labour, in other areas new defences were built with resources obtained from central government. At the same time heavy machinery from government agencies dredged the river and built dykes in accordance with the plans prepared by PREDES for the Frente.

While training courses continued with the different CBOs of the valley, the first half of 1985 saw an emphasis on consolidating the organisational process which was developing around the mitigation projects. Workshops on organisation, for community leaders, were set up by five second-tier CBOs and PREDES dealing with the internal problems of organisation, the relation between leaders and members and the relationship between CBOs and the state. Each second-tier CBO identified five leaders from their member organisations to participate in each workshop. The workshops used popular education methods in which leaders were encouraged to think together about real problems in order to increase their understanding of them and so be able to solve them. Three workshops were held, for 50 people. In addition, an education programme was carried out in schools to encourage young people to participate more actively in their own CBOs. Courses were developed with third, fourth and fifth year students on the following themes:

- **the disasters in Peru**
- **the historical evolution of the disasters**
- **the natural and social causes of the disasters**
- **disaster mitigation measures**
- **organisation for the prevention of disaster.**

A radio programme "El Huaico" was also broadcast weekly, to help the CBOs of the area in communicating with and educating the community.

The principal results of two years' intervention in the valley were:

1. A substantial strengthening and centralisation of community organisation in the area, with an increase in consciousness of the disaster problem and an improved capacity for negotiation with central government.
2. The implementation of a large number of local measures against floods and huaicos which reduced the immediate risk in many areas.
3. The investment of significant central government resources in CBO mitigation projects and the development of long term alternatives for vulnerability reduction in the area, which CBOs negotiated with central government.
4. The development of a number of techniques for flood defence and huaico control which could be undertaken and managed by people and their organisations, enabling local control over mitigation projects.

An Evaluation of the Experience

PIEVAR should be seen not just as an end in itself but as a pilot project with a much wider application. Important lessons were learnt as a result of carrying out the project. There are many factors which would be applicable in any situation where mitigation measures were to be carried out by community based organisations. Some of the most significant elements are summarised below.

Community Organisation

The experience of PIEVAR showed that community organisation is the single most important factor in hazard mitigation and vulnerability reduction. The project demonstrated that community based hazard mitigation is above all a gradual bottom-up process of changing the social, political and economic relationships between marginal groups and the state. The key to the success of the project lay in identifying mitigation as a major concern of the CBOs in the area which could unite them around a common programme of action.

The production of technical reports and studies, which CBOs could adopt as their own and use in negotiations with government authorities; the development of technical and legal tools, which could enable CBOs to devise and control their own mitigation projects and the creation of opportunities for reflection and learning were all ways in which the project was able to support the consolidation of community organisation in the valley.

The result of the intervention was clear. At the outset of the project, individual CBOs passively accepted the relief aid which government agencies provided. After two years, coalitions of CBOs, with their own mitigation projects, negotiated effectively with central government for the resources they needed. The process of consolidation was uneven and evidently had a long way to go, but a qualitative change in direction had been established.

Mitigating Risk

In order to mobilise their own resources effectively and to negotiate projects and proposals with central government, CBOs in the area needed to analyse the problems they faced and to develop mitigation proposals which were not only technically effective but which were susceptible to local control and management.

The Risk Studies helped CBOs develop a critical consciousness of the problems faced in their own areas and in the valley as a whole. In many areas CBOs carried out measures with their own resources. In other areas, CBOs were able to attract an unprecedented amount of resources from central government. After two years, the immediate risk in many areas had already been substantially reduced, while the future implementation of planned projects such as the channelling of the river would lead to a real reduction in the vulnerability of the whole area.

Throughout the development of the project, the mitigation measures increased in comprehensiveness by including new areas and integrating

The mitigation measures maximised the use of local resources and appropriate technology. These river defences use traditional methods and were planned and constructed by the community.

Andrew Maskrey/Juvenal Medina/Predes

new factors. Given the bottom-up process of community organisation, the analysis of problems and the development of proposals also had to be gradual and incremental - responding to the actual capabilities of the CBOs. This kind of planning was completely different from the large scale comprehensive planning common to large agencies.

Appropriate Technology

At the start of the project there was a general assumption amongst the CBOs of the area that mitigation required large scale technology managed by experts in centralised bureaucracies. CBOs had little confidence in their own resources of local materials and in their own capacity to manage projects.

The technical assistance and training aspects of the project were essential in that they helped to restore people's confidence in themselves by showing that mitigation could be just as effective without heavy plant and machinery, reinforced concrete and engineers.

The mitigation measures that were planned maximised the use of local resources and were on a scale that CBOs themselves could manage. This did not mean that only small self-help measures were possible. Comprehensive flood defence measures covering large areas were implemented, coordinated through a second-tier CBO but carried out by a number of first-tier CBOs. The use of local resources such as stone enabled far more defences to be built and the resources obtained from central government could then be used much more effectively.

Incremental Growth

The project evolved gradually over the two years both in scale and depth. New geographical areas and organisations were gradually incorporated as the team built up knowledge of the area and the problems which it faced. This is in contrast to the methodology usually adopted by large government agencies and NGOs, which establish large scale programmes right from the start. Building up gradually allowed the growth of the project to respond to the growth of the CBO movement, ensuring that the project always responded to people's own real needs and problems.

The sum of small scale actions, implemented by local CBOs but coordinated through a central plan managed by second-tier CBOs, demonstrated an efficiency greater than that of large scale projects managed from outside.

The role of the NGO

The role of the NGO was crucial to the development of this process. PREDES acted as an independent advisor to the CBOs. It neither attempted to substitute for the state by taking on the role of resource allocation or the implementation of mitigation projects, nor did it attempt to act as a representative for the CBOs. PREDES provided support to the CBOs according to their own needs and demands, and developed alternative solutions which the CBOs themselves could negotiate with the state. In this respect it is important that PREDES made it clear from the start that it was not a funding agency for CBOs, although it acted on several occasions as legal guarantor of funds obtained by them from government or other agencies.

The intervention of PREDES was only possible through a long period of building up trust, confidence and friendship between members of the team and local people and their leaders. This in turn was only possible because PREDES was a locally based NGO with a permanent presence in the area.

Building Confidence

Rather than generating dependency, the project built up the capacity of people and their CBOs to manage and negotiate their own programmes. Right from the start, leaders were responsible for activities such as convening assemblies, organising public works and selecting people for workshops. Initially PREDES assisted individual NGOs in their negotiations with the state and in the implementation of their own mitigation measures. However, more and more responsibility was gradually devolved to the CBOs themselves. The second-tier CBOs became responsible for the local coordination of activities between their member organisations.

A Multisectorial Approach

Because PREDES had a permanent presence in the area it was able to integrate mitigation into all phases of the disaster: emergency, recovery, reconstruction and preparedness. While not losing its specificity as an organisation which specialised in disasters, it was able to support different CBO programmes such as the obtaining of land titles and drinking water. This multisectorial approach to working corresponds far more closely to people's real needs and demands than the unisectorial programmes implemented by large agencies which do not have the flexibility to adapt to local conditions.

PREDES developed non-hierarchical management structures and interdisciplinary teams to implement the project. Small teams made up of people from different disciplines allowed a flexible response to problems which overflowed rigid disciplinary boundaries.

The Development of Methodology

The use of an action/research methodology was an important component in the project. It allowed the development of both innovative ways of studying and techniques for mitigating disaster, which were later applied successfully in other parts of the country. It also allowed the development of a general methodology for supporting CBO's mitigation programmes. As such, the project was a learning process for PREDES too.

The project demonstrated how disaster can become an effective stimulus for development when mitigation is under the control of local community organisations. The strengthening of community organisation, the development of alternative solutions to the disaster problem and the appropriation of technologies for mitigation enabled CBOs to move gradually from small ad hoc measures to mitigate specific risks towards obtaining substantial commitments from the state to permanently reducing vulnerability.

Five days of continuous rain led to landslips such as this one and resulted in the huaico which devastated Cuyocuyo in January 1984.

Andrew Maskrey/Juvenal Medina/Predes

Chapter Eight
THE RECOVERY OF CUYOCUYO
Introduction
The Rimac Valley project saw the development of a methodology for studying and a technology for mitigating huaico risk with the participation of local communities. In Cuyocuyo these were put into practice in an area with fewer constraints to mitigation and where the community maintained a level of autonomy from the state in the management of land and other resources. The results were exceptional.

The Disaster
In January 1984, Cuyocuyo, a small town situated 3200m above sea level between the southern highlands and the Amazon jungle, was devastated by a large huaico, following five consecutive days of rains. One third of the town's houses were completely destroyed together with its drinking water and electricity supplies, while the remaining areas were buried under a mass of mud and rock.

The peasant farmers and seasonal gold miners who form the community of Cuyocuyo are organised according to Peruvian law for rural areas. The Governor represents the state and is appointed by the government in power. The Mayor is locally elected and is in charge of local administration. The Justice of Peace represents the judicial system. Nonetheless, for the inhabitants of Cuyocuyo there is only one person in the town who has sufficient authority to be able to assemble and mobilise all the population. The Teniente 'Llacta'(a Quechua Indian word meaning community) has no legal or official recognition. His authority is sustained only by the tradition and respect of his own people. He does not need to read and write, is elected every two years in an assembly of all the adults in the community and is given authority to resolve disputes over land and marriage, to organise the start of the farming year and the harvesting of crops and to deal with all the problems which affect the community.

It was ten days after the disaster before Peruvian Civil Defence got through with tents, clothes and food. Apart from cleaning the mud out of their houses, people did little. Most were afraid of a repetition of the disaster. For many villagers the disaster was God's punishment for diverse cases of adultery and immoral behaviour. For others it was a clear indication that Cuyocuyo should be abandoned. In addition, a well meant but misunderstood offer by a foreign relief agency to rebuild the town with prefabricated housing further persuaded people just to sit back and wait. Cuyocuyo's legal authorities meanwhile were using their influences to obtain aid from the Government. The regional development corporation promised to send materials and heavy plant to rebuild the town and construct defences. This offer also encouraged people to wait.

Six months after the disaster, a relief agency asked a team from PREDES to study the causes of the disaster and to make recommendations for rebuilding. After a few day's field work the team concluded that the causes of the disaster were oversaturated hillside terraces, which had collapsed into a flooded mountain river a few kilometres upstream from Cuyocuyo. Unless the river was channelled between stone walls for a length of five kilometres and unless irrigation channels were rebuilt, the disaster could repeat itself on a bigger scale the following year. These conclusions were presented to a communal assembly presided over by the Teniente Llacta and, despite the titanic nature of the works required, it was decided that in a space of three months the defences could be built using local materials and techniques and with the participation of men and women from the whole community.

For 30 consecutive days, under the direction of the Teniente Llacta and following the plans drawn up by PREDES, 120 men and women worked eight hours a day to finish ten kilometres of two metre high retaining wall on the river. Although the much vaunted prefabricated housing and heavy plant had still not arrived, Cuyocuyo was now better protected and while in 1985 the rains were heavier than the year before, no further disaster occurred.

The Evaluation of the Experience

As in the Rimac valley, the causes of the disaster could be traced back to historical processes. The town of Cuyocuyo is located in the valley bottom, vulnerable to both floods and huaicos. The settlements of the indigenous peasants, on the other hand, are all on high ground in secure locations. In Cuyocuyo, families traditionally farmed land in four different altitudinal zones to guarantee a variety of production and protection against hazard such as drought, frost and blights. However, this ecological balance had been disturbed. For many families in Cuyocuyo, farming is now a secondary activity. The men of the community migrate annually to mine gold in the jungle of Madre de Dios. Cuyocuyo is firmly integrated into the money economy and many

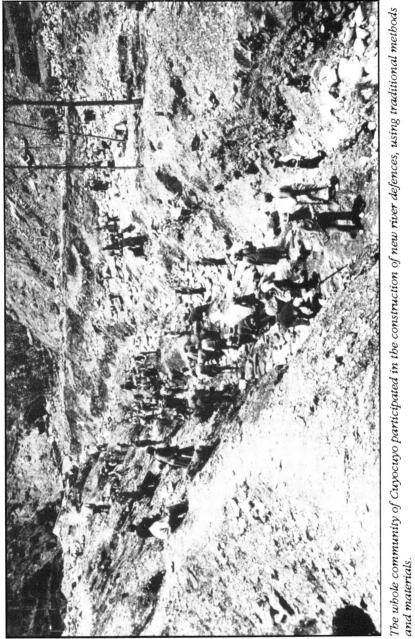

The whole community of Cuyocuyo participated in the construction of new river defences, using traditional methods and materials.

Andrew Maskrey/Juvenal Medina/Predes

families have comparatively high incomes for a rural area.

The root causes of the disaster were the founding of a colonial town by the Spanish in a vulnerable location and the gradual abandoning of traditional agricultural practices. One of the immediate causes of the disaster was the lack of maintenance of irrigation channels, with the result that water overflowed onto an exposed hillside. The huaico of January 1984 was the first in living memory, but in many ways an inevitable consequence of centuries of change.

Although, after the disaster, the level of risk in Cuyocuyo was very high, as an even larger huaico could easily occur the following year, the people were less vulnerable than many communities in the Rimac valley. Despite the economic changes of recent years, the community maintained a strong organisational tradition, and was not poor. The community itself controlled virtually all the local resources in the area and being isolated was highly self-reliant. People had an excellent grasp of traditional techniques of wall and house building using local stone.

The community's first response to the disaster was conditioned by the cultural and political domination of the local authorities (Governor, Mayor, Justice of the Peace) who monopolised all contacts with the state and other outside agencies. They were dismissive of indigenous culture and lifestyle and wanted a 'modern' and 'civilised' recovery from the disaster, symbolised by the use of heavy machinery and prefabricated building. The promises of aid from both the Government and an international aid agency effectively inhibited any local recovery efforts for the first six months.

If the official plan to 'modernise' Cuyocuyo had actually been implemented, in the long run the vulnerability of the community would have been increased, because the last vestiges of autonomous organisation and ecological balance which still existed in the area would have been destroyed. Nor would the immediate risk have been removed. The huaico was formed on a hillside four kilometres away and 1000 metres above Cuyocuyo. Reinforced concrete defence walls in the valley bottom, which the Government had promised to build, would have made little difference. The government authorities were inherently unable to mitigate risk in Cuyocuyo because they could not mobilise the resources available in the local community itself - organisation, labour, local technology and local materials - and relied on a top-down approach to mitigation using disabling and inappropriate technologies. The well known international aid agency arrived in Cuyocuyo with altruistic and humanitarian motives but by making contact only with the authorities, unwittingly fell into the same trap.

PREDES did nothing new or original in Cuyocuyo, but simply put into practice the methods and techniques developed in the upper Rimac valley. A team of three professionals (a town planner, a geologist and a forestry engineer) carried out two weeks' field work to determine the causes of the disaster and design mitigation measures. Unlike the Government's plans, all the measures proposed could be undertaken by local people with the resources and techniques they had at hand. Only part of the work required cement, which people would have to obtain by negotiating with government. Both the short term measures (the stone walls) and long term measures to improve soil and water management and thus reduce vulnerability in the future, involved work being carried out high up on the mountainside, where bulldozers could not be used. To be effective, the measures depended on people working together cooperatively, so needed to be under the control of the local community itself.

PREDES worked directly with the local community and it was local people through their own authority, the Teniente Llacta, who took the decision to carry out the recovery programme. The risk study was a small investment, costing only a few hundred dollars, but it mobilised a community and its resources for three months, which no amount of money invested in a top down programme could have achieved.

While the mitigation measures implemented were impressive in scale and worked in practice, they also strengthened community organisation. The community regained confidence in itself and in its own technology and culture. A second PREDES team spent three months in Cuyocuyo giving technical assistance to the community to complete the measures and to make use of the experience to build up organisation and consciousness, working with local schools and CBOs. The maintenance of the organisational level achieved and an increase in awareness was essential if the medium and long term mitigation measures were to be implemented and the walls maintained.* This task was carried on by TECIRA, a local NGO, on the basis of the PREDES study. Right from the start, PREDES had made it clear that only a local NGO could take on the long term responsibility for supporting the development of the area.

An interesting facet of the experience is the way aid was used. Once the immediate emergency had passed, food aid brought in by the aid agency and by the Government had been a major factor in keeping the community passive and dependent on the authorities. Aid was a demobilising factor. After the community's recovery programme was launched, the food was used for the workers building the defence walls on the hill side and became a positive factor, enabling people to give up three months of their time to mitigation. Armed with their own technical study and supported by their own advisors, people were able to use government cement and machinery to support and complete their own efforts. Events had taken a very different turn.

Finally, the cost effectiveness of the programme can be illustrated by the fact that, after all the objectives had been fully met, PREDES was able to return two thirds of the funds provided by the aid agency for the recovery programme and for which PREDES had been acting as guarantor.

* Author's note: We now (1989) know that the medium and long term mitigation measures were never properly implemented. It also appears that maintenance of the short term mitigation measure (the river canalisation) was not carried out. Because of this a further huaico occurred in Cuyocuyo in 1988 causing new losses. In our opinion, this information, which was unavailable when the case study was written up, only serves to confirm the need for long term inputs, based on supporting and building up CBOs, if short term mitigation is to become a vehicle for long term vulnerability reduction.

Chapter Nine

MITIGATION PROGRAMMES IN OTHER CONTEXTS

The Programmes

The case studies from Peru show the advantages of community based disaster mitigation over conventional top down programmes. These advantages can be seen in perspective by analysing 14 mitigation programmes from different countries. The commentaries on the programmes only refer to the information available in the documents quoted. Naturally, they do not necessarily reflect the definitive version of events, nor do they hope to give a complete picture. However, it is possible to divide the programmes into two kinds, those that illustrate the conventional top down approach to mitigation and those that illustrate the community based approach, and compare the effectiveness of these approaches.

Top Down Programmes

1. BOLIVIA - Altiplano - *Programa de Refinanciamiento del Banco Central de Bolivia - 1983*

Kind of Hazard - Drought

Character - This was a recovery programme after the drought of 1983. Special credits were provided at an interest of 10% below the normal rate for the recovery of the production of crops such as maize, wheat, rice and potatoes. The programme was directed to individual peasants affected by the drought. Its objectives were to reduce migration to the cities and food importation by restoring production.

Agents - The programme was financed and implemented by the Banco Central de Bolivia and aimed at individual producers.

Results - It was hoped to finance 142,945 Has. of cultivation. Only 31.64% of this total was achieved and the departments worst hit by the drought, Oruro and Potosi, only obtained 7.2% of the credits.

Lessons - The project did not benefit those most in need: landless and poor peasants. They were too poor to receive the credits. Also they were afraid of planting using credit in case of another drought which would leave them in debt and with the risk of having their land confiscated.

Source - PRUDENCIO, Julio, 'La Sequia en Bolivia: 1982 - 1983', in *Desastres y Sociedad en America Latina*, Grupo Editora Latinoamericana, Buenos Aires, 1985.

2. BOLIVIA - *Altiplano* - *Plan de Emergencia del Gobierno Boliviano* - *1983*

Kind of Hazard - Drought

Objectives - This was the National Emergency Plan of the Bolivian Government during the 1983 drought. It consisted of different measures: amplifying the winter agricultural campaign to new areas not affected by the drought; rescuing and importing potato seed for the campaign of the following year; the provision of water supplies to rural communities and their livestock and the distribution of emergency food supplies.

Agents - The plan was coordinated by the National Civil Defence Committee and incorporated different government and voluntary agencies. It had no coordination with CSUTB, the Bolivian Confederation of Peasants' Unions, the principal organisation which represented rural communities.

Results - Only 23% of the proposed winter agricultural campaign was achieved. At the rural level the results were almost nil. No wells were dug and the rescue of potato seeds was not carried out. The water programme was implemented only in the urban area of Potosi. However, the food distribution programme under the control of voluntary agencies was more effective.

Lessons - This ambitious centrally planned programme failed due to a lack of participation of local community organisations and a mismatch between the objectives and general analysis made at central level and specific and variable local conditions. Added to those factors was the disorganisation of the public sector and the lack of the necessary resources and infrastructure to put the plan into action. Due to its centralist approach, the programme wasted most of the few resources it had available.

Source - PRUDENCIO, Julio, *Op. Cit.*

3. BRAZIL - North East (Sertao) - Programa de Emergencia en las Sequias - 1979-1980

Kind of Hazard - Drought

Character - This was the Government's Drought Emergency Programme of 1979 - 1980 in north-east Brazil. The objective of the programme was to increase agricultural production and use of land by dynamising the economy of the region and integrating it into national and international markets. The programme consisted of credits to land owners to improve productivity and the quality of products on their farms.

Agents - The programme was carried out by the Inspector of Works Against the Drought (IOCS - Inspectora de Obras contra as Secas).

Results - There was a wide difference between the objectives of the programme and the results obtained. The population of the region was assumed to be homogeneous, without social and economic differences between different groups. The criteria for participating in the programme directly benefited the richer and least affected groups and excluded the worst affected (i.e. landless peasants and labourers). The vulnerability of these groups increased and they ended up poorer and more dependent than before the programme.

Lessons - The Government used a drought programme with an apparently neutral aim (increasing productivity) to benefit dominant groups with political power and economic resources, worsening the conditions of the most affected.

Source - PANDOLFI, Maria Lia, 'Brasil: Programa de Emergencia en las Sequias de 1979 - 1980', in *Desastres y Sociedad en America Latina*, Buenos Aires, 1985.

4. HONDURAS - Sulla Valley - Reconstruction Programme after Hurricane Fifi

Kind of Hazard - Hurricane

Character - This was a reconstruction programme after Hurricane Fifi, which struck the north coast of Honduras in 1974. It consisted of the construction of 350 houses in 3 new settlements for people whose homes had been destroyed by floods and mudslides.

Agents - The project was financed and implemented by two ecumenical associations (one from the United States and a Honduran counterpart). Land for the new settlements was provided by the INA (Instituto Nacional Agraria), a government agency, and two local municipalities.

Results - Three settlements were formed: San Jose; Santa Rita and Flores de Oriente. They were built with new construction materials such as reinforced concrete but two of the settlements were located in areas vulnerable to new floods and landslides.

Lessons - In the reconstruction programme, the main causal factor of the disaster, location, had been ignored. The local and central government agencies which provided the sites could only direct people back to vulnerable locations. On the other hand, the emphasis on heavy construction was expensive and largely unnecessary.

Source - SNARR, BROWN, 'Permanent Post Disaster Housing in Honduras: Aspects of Vulnerability to Future Disasters', *Disasters* Vol 3. No.3, 1979.

5. NICARAGUA - Managua - Reconstruction programme, 1972

Kind of Hazard - Earthquake

Character - This was the Government's reconstruction programme for Managua after the 1972 earthquake. The central zone of Managua was forcibly evacuated, later demolished and never rebuilt. Other public works reconstruction programmes existed, however, for repaving roads for instance.

Agents - The programme was carried out by central government. The evacuation was enforced by the National Guard with support from the US army. Most reconstruction works were implemented by companies owned by the President or his associates. The population had no level of social organisation or participation. $57 million were received in aid mainly from the United States.

Results - Only $16 million dollars of aid were ever properly accounted for. No provision was made for rebuilding for the 350,000 people who were evacuated from Managua. Foreign aid and reconstruction was used by Government and National Guard as an opportunity for making large illicit profits. The resulting social polarisation contributed to the 1979 revolution.

Lessons - Aid is not important in itself, but how it is used. When it is channelled through an oppressive and corrupt regime it is used to make the rich richer and not to help those most affected by disaster. However, such abuses may eventually lead to radical change.

Source - BOMMER, Julian, *Op. Cit.*

6. PAKISTAN - Patan - Recovery and reconstruction after the 1974 earthquake

Kind of Hazard - Earthquake

Character - This was the Government reconstruction programme following the 1974 earthquake. Grants were made available for the reconstruction of housing by people themselves. Plans and surveys were also carried out for the relocation of the town in a safe area.

Agents - The programme was implemented by the Kohistan Development Board and other government agencies. £24 million of foreign aid was received, mainly from Arab countries.

Results - People gave higher priority to agricultural recovery than to the rapid reconstruction of their homes. As no technical assistance was made available with the credits, many of the reconstructed houses were more vulnerable than the original pre-earthquake structures. The relocation plan took so long to complete, that it was precluded by people's own reconstruction activities.

Lessons - Credits for reconstruction need to be accompanied by training in building techniques right from the start. Ambitious relocation and reconstruction plans which take years to elaborate only serve to demobilise and demoralise people, creating expectations that are later not fulfilled.

Source - DAVIS, Ian, 'Analysis of Recovery and Reconstruction Following the 1974 Patan Earthquake', in *International Karakorum Project*, Cambridge University Press, 1984.

7. PERU - Ancash - Reconstruction of Huaraz and the Callejon de Huaylas

Kind of Hazard - Earthquake

Character - This was the Government reconstruction programme in Huaraz, carried out after the 1970 earthquake. The programme consisted of the construction of new housing and the reconstruction and rehabilitation of infrastructure. Seismogeological zoning was undertaken as the basis for a new town plan, land was expropriated and credits were given for new housing.

Agents - The project was implemented by CRYRZA (Comite de Reconstruccion y Rehabilitacion de la Zona Afectada) and later by ORDEZA, a regional development agency. The project was funded mainly by US Aid and the World Bank. Total aid in the earthquake zone by 1977 totalled over $30 million.

Results - Three years were spent on the seismogeological zoning. By this time people had already begun reconstruction on their own, making the zoning and resulting plan irrelevant. While the plan was being drawn up, reconstruction in the city centre was banned, meaning that people were forced to erect precarious housing in marginal vulnerable areas. The regulatory plan was only half completed. Credits for housing were only available to middle class people and not to those worst affected. Priority was given to reconstructing productive infrastructure and public buildings.

Lessons - Central government projects with large investments often do nothing to help the majority worst affected by disaster. Funds are channelled towards the better off and towards the public and private sectors. Planning becomes irrelevant, no matter how sophisticated it is, when it fails to take into account the needs and priorities of the majority and ignores and fails to support people's own efforts to rebuild and recover.

Source - SAGAV, Margo, 'The Interface between Earthquake Planning and Development Planing: A Case Study and Critique of the Reconstruction of Huaraz and the Callejon de Huaylas, Ancash, Peru, Following the 31 May 1970 Earthquake', *Disasters*, Vol.3, No.3, 1979.

8. PERU - Chiclayo - Reconstruction project after the 1983 floods

Kind of Hazard - Flood

Character - This was a programme of housing reconstruction following the floods in northern Peru in 1983. The project consisted of the reconstruction of a village with houses of stabilised adobe, with the objective of mitigating the effects of future floods. The implementing agencies supplied local people with building materials and technical assistance. People themselves were to build the houses.

Agents - The project was implemented by the Development Corporation of the Department of Lambayeque, a regional development agency. Technical assistance was given by the Universidad Catolica de Peru. Financial support was from US AID.

Results - The project was only partially completed. People were sceptical about the new technology and did not like the house designs, which were drawn up without their participation. People also gave more priority to recovering agricultural production and repairing irrigation infrastructure than to house building.

Lessons - Well meaning and technically adequate mitigation measures may be irrelevant to the needs and priorities of the people, when there has been no participation in their design. Project implementation becomes extremely difficult when authority is not vested in people's own legitimate organisations.

Source - TORREALVA, Daniel, 'A Reconstruction Project in Chiclayo Peru After the 1983 Floods', International Conference on Disaster Mitigation Program Implementation, Jamaica, 1984.

Characteristics of Top Down Programmes

A general characteristic of the government programmes was that those worst affected by disaster, who had little possibility of recovery, received least benefit. In fact some programmes (1. Bolivia, 3. Brazil and 7. Peru) explicitly sought to benefit social groups that were relatively unaffected, those with political power and economic resources; landowners, rich peasants in unaffected areas or urban property owners with stable incomes. Poor, landless peasants, farm labourers or marginal urban dwellers with low or irregular incomes were excluded from the programmes. On the whole, as a result of the programmes they found themselves living in more precarious and fragile conditions, more vulnerable to future disaster. Only two programmes, 2. Bolivia and 6. Pakistan, actually attempted to benefit those worst affected by the disasters.

Two of the programmes, 1. Bolivia and 3. Brazil, based on rural credit, were explicitly designed to protect the economic interests of a dominant minority rather than to improve conditions for those worst affected by the disaster. For instance, the objective of one programme (1. Bolivia) was to avoid rural-urban migration. However, from the point of view of those affected this may have been the most logical survival strategy to avoid further disaster. In the same programme many peasants refused to receive credit at all because of the risk of building up debt and having their land confiscated, a disaster potentially worse than drought. For the supposed beneficiaries the remedy appeared worse than the disease.

Vulnerability emerges through changes in local, regional and national economies, and some programmes deliberately accelerated those changes, making vulnerability worse. Such programmes did not merely attack the symptoms rather than the causes of vulnerability; they aggravated the causes. In one programme (3. Brazil) agriculture for the market was promoted rather than agriculture for subsistence, directly benefiting large landowners who could improve productivity and marginalising small farmers and landless peasants who could not. A less subtle form of making the vulnerable majority worse off is corruption. This was evident in one form or another in several programmes.

Political motives had an important influence in the mitigation programmes (2. Bolivia, 6. Pakistan and 7. Peru). The need to establish the credibility of the governing party; forthcoming elections; establishing a good international image and even the political promotion of individuals were elements which explain the character of many programmes. Comparable motives may influence the donation of aid at an international level (5. Nicaragua).

Such political objectives were rarely explicit, however; they were often hidden beneath a technocratic disguise. For example, in 7. Peru and 6. Pakistan, seismogeological zoning studies were used apparently to decide new land uses but actually these served political and economic interests; in 3. Brazil the need to modernise agriculture gave an air of neutrality to a credit programme for rich landowners.

Irrespective of their economic and political objectives, government mitigation programmes were characterised by their inefficiency. Because they were centrally controlled, planned and implemented they were unable to take into account the variability of local needs and conditions and failed to meet their goals and fell short of their targets in many cases. Their ineffectiveness meant that the few resources available for mitigation were absorbed by bureaucracy or wasted in actions which did not achieve their objectives.

The programmes were almost inevitably unisectorial, dealing with single factors such as agricultural credit, rural infrastructure, house building or public works. They dealt with only one phase of a disaster: emergency, recovery or reconstruction. They were unable to take into account the complexity of people's needs.

The ineffectiveness of even well-intentioned government programmes was largely due to their failure to recognise and work through CBOs. In some programmes (5. Nicaragua) CBOs were considered subversive. In others (2. Bolivia) they were simply ignored. The programmes were unable to tap the biggest resource available for disaster mitigation, people themselves and their organisations, with their own intimate knowledge of local conditions and culture.

Many programmes legitimised and perpetuated themselves by using centralised methods and techniques to study and mitigate risk. This gave more power to large organisations and experts and at the same time led to measures which did not respond to people's real needs. The time that studies took to complete meant that they were obsolete before they were finished. Sometimes they generated expectations which were never fulfilled, but which meanwhile discouraged people's own mitigation initiatives, as in 7. Peru.

Unlike governments, international and national NGOs do try to direct their programmes to benefit those worst affected by disaster and with least possibility of recuperating. However, although they may have altruistic objectives they do not necessarily produce effective results or meet the real needs and priorities of the intended beneficiaries.

One of the programmes examined (4. Honduras) was a conventional reconstruction programme which showed the NGOs acting as surrogates for government. As the allocation of land for the programme was still the responsibility of municipal and government authorities, the programme was faced with the same limitations and constraints which characterised the government programmes. In two of the three settlements rebuilt, land was allocated in locations proven to be vulnerable. The programme was limited because it could not affect the structure of land ownership (one of the causes of the disaster), only construction, which was not a problem.

A recurrent problem in all the NGO programmes was that, like government agencies, international and even national NGOs were not necessarily familiar with local conditions and culture. Similar mistakes were made. Programmes did not always correspond to people's own priorities or take into account the importance of local tradition and culture. The programmes were unisectorial. They prioritised housing, for example in 8. Peru, although help with this was not necessarily people's first need. Some programmes were unable to persuade people to participate because they had no real links with CBOs. Implementing became impossible because authority was not vested in people themselves, their leaders and organisations.

Problems also occurred with training. Unlike government programmes which completely excluded people's own unaided reconstruction efforts, NGOs tried to support those efforts through training. However, people were unable to act on the knowledge transmitted because of economic or cultural constraints. Without the participation of CBOs in the design and organisation of training programmes, these can fall into a social vacuum.

Community Based Programmes

9. BOLIVIA - La Paz, Oruro, Potosí, Tarija - *Programa de Recuperacion Agropecuaria Campesina - PRACA*

Kind of hazard - Drought

Character - PRACA was the Programa de Recuperacion Agropecuaria Campesina, carried out after the drought of 1983 in the altiplano of Bolivia. It consisted of organisational, educational and technical support to peasant communities in the areas worst affected by the drought. Different projects were promoted: traditional crops; alternative and experimental crops; forestation; colonisation of new land and animal health. The programme worked through reinforcing peasant organisation, introducing new agricultural practices and technical assistance.

Agents - PRACA was formed by a group of Bolivian NGOs which already had projects in the area (ACLO, IPTK PIO XII, SEMTA, CIPCA, QHANA) together with sectors of the Church. The NGOs elaborated and coordinated a joint plan. All the projects were implemented through local agreements with peasant communities.

Results - The programme covered 1,200 communities with a population of 50,000 families. There were significant advances in all the activities planned. Results were better in areas where the peasants had communal ownership of the land.

Lessons - It is possible to change agricultural practices and carry out extensive programmes when responsibility is vested in people's own organisations and their legitimate authorities. A group of local small NGOs can achieve significant results and cover a large geographic and demographic area when they coordinate and programme actions together.

Source - PRACA, *Programa de Recuperacion Agropecuaria Campesina - PRACA*, La Paz, Bolivia, 1986.

10. ECUADOR - Cuenca Baja del Guayas - Plan de Emergencia de UNOCOVB - 1982-1983

Kind of Hazard - Flood

Character - This was an emergency programme planned and executed by UNOCAVB (Union de Organizaciones Campesina de Vinces-Baba) in the wake of the floods of 1982-1983. It consisted of: distribution of food supplies; agricultural recovery and a health programme. The programme attempted to attack the immediate problems of hunger and illness through promoting an agricultural recovery based on the peasants' own organisation and the strengthening of this organisation through the incorporation of new groups. The plan was initiated because government and aid agencies were operating only in accessible urban areas.

Agents - The programme was carried out by UNOCAVB, which represented 30 peasants' organisations and had 10 years of work in the area. CEPI, a committee of NGOs provided financial support.

Results - The results were positive. Approximately 35,000 people were helped. The distribution of aid was efficient, orderly and honest, handled through 218 local committees, controlled by weekly assemblies. Fourteen health committees were set up. Three support teams made up of agronomists and community leaders gave technical assistance. UNOCAVB supported 100 other peasant organisations which were not members of the union, to generate solidarity.

Lessons - When material aid is controlled by CBOs it can be used very positively. When people are organised, they can respond effectively to an emergency. That response also helps to strengthen organisation.
"In this sense, the emergency and the mobilisation of peasants from the Cuenca de Guayas demonstrated that the disaster victims' own and legitimate organisation, when it is popular (without mechanisms of external control), has an efficiency, which is incomparably better than other, paternalistic efforts."

Source - EGAS, A. Raul, 'Ecuador: Inundaciones 1982 - 1983 en la Cuenca Baja del Guayas: Procesos de Organizacion de los Campesinos para hacer Frente al Desastre', in *Desastres Naturales y Sociedad en America Latina*, Grupo Editora Latinoamericana, 1985.

11. EL SALVADOR - San Salvador - Emergency programme following 1986 earthquake

Kind of Hazard - Earthquake

Character - This was an emergency programme which was implemented immediately (three hours) after the 1986 earthquake. It consisted of estimating damage and material needs; organising emergency committees, where people did not already have community organisations; donation of materials and tools for the removal of debris; the construction of temporary shelter and technical assistance to determine the danger of collapsing buildings. All materials and tools were handled and distributed by community organisations who had responsibility for determining needs.

Agent - The project was implemented by a national NGO, FUNDASAL (Fundacion Salvadorena de Desarollo y Vivienda Minima), which had worked for years in the area. All the actions were carried out by local community organisations and emergency committees with support from the NGO.

Results - The programme helped 113,000 people in 85 communities in the emergency phase. The work with the communities allowed criteria for the reconstruction to be formulated and which were accepted by other institutions.

Lessons - FUNDASAL was able to act quickly because it was already working in the slum area affected by the earthquake. However, the effectiveness and coverage of the programme was due to the responsibility being vested in community organisations.

Sources - FUNDASAL, *Primera Aproximacion de la Respuesta de la Fundacion Salvadorena de Desarollo y Vivienda Minima a la Emergencia Causada por el Terremoto del 10 de Octubre de 1986*, El Salvador, 1986.
FUNDASAL, *Despues de la Emergencia: Necesidad de una Politica de Vivienda Popular a Mediano y Largo Plazo*, El Salvador, 1986.

12. MOZAMBIQUE - *Flood prevention and mitigation*

Kind of Hazard - Floods

Character - This programme was the resettlement of rural and urban population from areas of high risk to areas of low risk, accompanied by physical protection measures such as dykes, reforestation and watershed control. The programme was based on the organisation and raising of the political consciousness of the rural population together with the assignment of land to landless peasants.

Agents - The project was carried out by the Government and by popular organisations.

Results - The main result was the resettlement of 500,000 peasants from areas of high flood risk to areas of low flood risk. This was complemented by flood control, watershed management and urban floodplain management carried out in different areas being incorporated into a comprehensive land-use management system.

Lessons - A process of political mobilisation and organisation of the population can make people less vulnerable. Within this process, risk to flood hazard is also mitigated. A precondition for this change in Mozambique was the 1976 revolution.

Source - WISNER, Ben, 'Flood Prevention and Mitigation in the Peoples Republic of Mozambique', *Disasters* Vol.3, No.3, 1979.

13. NICARAGUA - *Chinandega - Response to floods in western Nicaragua, 1982*

Kind of Hazard - Flood

Character - This was the emergency response to floods in western Nicaragua in 1982. The response consisted in rescue operations, emergency health programmes and the organisation of the initial stages of the recovery.

Agents - The programme was implemented by the Comites de Defensa Sandinista (CDS) of the area in coordination with military and government agencies. The CDS are an important level of community organisation, trained for military defence. Very little international aid was received, considering the magnitude of the disaster.

Results - Response to the disaster was well organised and effective. Despite enormous material damage only 80 people were killed. (In a much smaller disaster in Honduras in a similar area, 210 people were killed.) However, lack of specific training in natural disaster preparedness hindered the efficiency of the emergency operations.

Lessons - Strong local organisation is the key to an effective response to disaster, can greatly reduce casualties and losses and can lead to a speedy recovery. However, organisation must be complemented by specific training in disaster preparedness.

Source - BOMMER, Julian, 'The Politics of Disaster: Nicaragua', *Disasters* Vol.9 No.4, 1985.

14. PERU - Puno - Drought Relief and Community Agricultural Development Programme

Kind of Hazard - Drought and Flood

Character - This was a Drought Relief and Community Agricultural Development Programme in areas of the Peruvian altiplano which were affected by drought in 1983 and then by flood in 1986. After the drought an emergency programme was set up to work with peasant organisations, creating a revolving fund for seed distribution to guarantee the next agricultural campaign. Technical assistance was also given The emergency programme gave way to an agricultural development programme consisting of studies, training and technical assistance for: irrigation using pumped underground water; the identification of flood risk areas; the creation of family vegetable plots and the improvement of irrigation canals.

Agents - The programme was planned and implemented by CEPIA (Centro de Proyectos Integrales en Base a la Alpaca) a local NGO which had worked in the area for several years, in coordination with the peasant communities of the area. HIVOS and Oxfam gave financial support. The Ministry of Agriculture had to give permission for the use of underground water, which delayed the actions.

Results - Because the revolving fund was managed by peasant organisations themselves, the level of repayment was far higher than with conventional government credit programmes. The programme reinforced organisation and encouraged peasants to take up more efficient communal farming practices.

Lessons - Material aid and credit can be used positively when it is under the control of local organisations. The programme also shows how disaster can be an opportunity to reinforce organisation and to improve traditional farming practices.

Source - CEPIA, *Proyecto Desarollo Agricola: Informe Actividades, Octobre 1985 - Abril 1986*, Peru, 1986.
CEPIA, *Proyecto Emergencia Agricola Informe de Actividades, Enero - Diciembre 1984*, Peru, 1985.

Characteristics of Community Based Programmes

There are few documented case studies illustrating the community based approach to mitigation.

The definitive characteristic of all the programmes was that the principal responsibility and authority for the development of the programme rested with the CBO. Because CBOs are deeply rooted in the society and culture of each area, they enabled people to express their real needs and priorities, allowing problems to be correctly defined and responsive mitigation measures to be designed. Following disaster, people were able through CBOs to articulate strategies for recovery and reconstruction which responded to their real needs (9. Bolivia, 11. El Salvador).

The existence of CBOs also allowed people to respond to emergency situations rapidly and effectively. In various cases (10. Ecuador, 11. El Salvador and 13. Nicaragua) the distribution of emergency aid by CBOs was just and efficient, eliminating bureaucratic delays and corruption. An interesting comparison with the top down approach is that in one programme (14. Peru) the CBO itself managed a revolving credit fund, which did reach the intended beneficiaries and had a high rate of repayment.

All the cases highlight that the principal resource available for mitigating disaster is people themselves and their local knowledge and expertise. Through mobilising this resource all the programmes had relatively small financial inputs but were able to produce large scale results. Under the control of CBOs resources were used economically and effectively. Community based programmes were multisectorial, combining different activities, hazards and disaster phases (housing and agriculture; health and agriculture; drought and flood; emergency and recovery).

The support activities of NGOs were far more effective in community based programmes than in top down programmes. For example, 10. Ecuador and 9. Bolivia showed how technical assistance and training given served to reinforce and strengthen organisation, which in turn permitted the implementation of mitigation measures.

Many of the programmes (9, Bolivia, 10. Ecuador, 12. Mozambique and 14. Peru) showed how disaster can be a unique opportunity for change, bringing into focus problems which are normally obscured. Mitigation is a model which can stimulate organisation and allow people to experiment with new techniques and technologies.

While in all the cases risk to a specific hazard was mitigated, in none of the cases did the programme lead to a real change in the social, economic and political relations which underlie vulnerability. However, all the programmes reinforced organisation, building up consciousness, awareness and critical appraisal. In this way, they increased people's potential for reducing their vulnerability, in contrast to most of the top down programmes.

Community based programmes are not necessarily small scale. Four of the programmes (9. Bolivia, 11. El Salvador, 12. Mozambique and 13. Nicaragua) covered large geographical areas, with populations in excess of 100,000 people. One programme (9. Bolivia) is particularly important because it showed how a group of local NGOs could coordinate policy and planning over a large area, while each carried out specific local projects with CBOs within this agreed framework. This particular programme, supported by six local NGOs, covered 50,000 families (probably 300,000 people) in 1,200 different rural communities. Large coverage with small resources is possible through horizontal coordination and links between CBOs.

The most exciting programmes were those where the state supported and complemented CBO actions through a devolution of power and resources to the local level and the implementation of major economic and political reforms. In one case, 13. Nicaragua, loss of life in a major disaster was reduced drastically and the recovery accelerated. In another, 12. Mozambique, risk to flood was reduced by up to 50% at the national level, with the resettlement of 500,000 people in non-vulnerable areas. This programme is particularly interesting, given the difficulties of relocating even a few dozen people found in other contexts.

Critiques of Top Down Mitigation

Criticism of top down mitigation can be summarised under three main headings:

Failure to address vulnerability: Top down mitigation programmes managed by central government, international agencies or NGOs are almost always unisectorial, responding to one particular hazard type in a specific and limited time period. As such, they cannot address vulnerability, which is a complex relationship between people and their social, physical and economic environment. Because they ignore the enormous range and variety of local needs and priorities, even well-intentioned programmes are often counterproductive for low income people. Despite the collection of objective data on people's social and economic conditions and behavioural response to hazards, top down mitigation fails to take into account the complex range of factors which go to make up people's own decisions. While a programme might relocate people to reduce flood risk, at the same time it might expose them to more serious risks such as poverty and isolation.

Failure to involve people - Because of their reliance on specialised technologies and professional skills, top down mitigation programmes tend to be carried out without the involvement of local people and their organisations in planning and decision making. People's participation is reduced to providing labour in organised self-help schemes. Programmes are inherently uneconomic because they exclude the principal resources available for mitigation in most contexts: people themselves, their local knowledge, skills and organisation. Because they are unable to make use of these resources, top down mitigation programmes rarely achieve their objectives and often waste scarce external resources.

Susceptibility to manipulation - The third and most serious criticism of top down mitigation is that because of the concentration of power and knowledge amongst a centralised management, it is particularly susceptible to political manipulation by powerful groups, especially in the case of government programmes. Mitigation becomes an instrument for maintaining the status quo or for actually making the poor majority more vulnerable. For many governments, hazard mitigation is motivated more by political and economic self-interest than by humanitarian motives. In general, government mitigation programmes tend to limit demand-making by low income people and their organisations, either by outright repression or by cooption. Autonomous community organisation is controlled and inhibited and its role restricted to innocuous self-help activities, thus avoiding the emergence of political consciousness and any challenge to the existing power structure.

The Ideology of Top Down Mitigation

While most government programmes are essentially authoritarian in character, top down NGO programmes tend to be paternalistic but can be equally damaging to autonomous community organisation. Top down mitigation is regulated by a strong ideological control. Disaster has come to be synonymous with relief, and relief with large governmental and international agencies. Mitigation is associated with professionals and high technology and local know-how is distrusted. In top down programmes self-help and self-build do not represent any real devolution of power and resources to local people and their organisations.

The necessary conclusion is that top down mitigation does little to reduce the level of vulnerability faced by the poor majority. Instead it often serves the interests of rich and powerful groups and may even create conditions for increased vulnerability and further disaster.

Community Based Mitigation: An Evolving Practice

Governments respond more to political pressure than to reasoned arguments to change their policies, and that pressure can best be exerted by those who suffer the effects of disaster: people themselves and their own autonomous organisations or CBOs.

Faced with a multi-faceted daily disaster, CBOs have their own strategies for improving living conditions, obtaining greater access to resources and changing the character of social relations with other groups, particularly the state. CBO actions deal with a wide variety of problems: housing, health, agriculture, education and so on. Where natural hazards are a serious and frequent threat to lives, livelihoods and homes, then hazard mitigation can become important for CBOs. Only local people know their own needs and therefore only they can define their own priorities for mitigation, within a given context. CBOs do not act for abstract ideological reasons; specific local problems are always the motivation for their action. For many CBOs, mitigation is a permanent activity and an integral part of their survival strategies.

The form mitigation takes and the way it evolves depends on the context. In some 'traditional' contexts, where people and their organisations still have some control over their economic situation, there is often space for adjustment or adaptation to hazard. With increasing urbanisation and the break down of rural economies and social relations that goes with it, the space for adaption or adjustment becomes increasingly reduced as vulnerability becomes more extreme and develops new facets. CBO mitigation strategies in most contexts inevitably involve negotiation or confrontation with the state or market forces.

The mechanisms by which CBOs develop their strategies depend on the way in which they relate to government and other external agencies. CBOs mitigation practice evolves over time, with periods of integration, participation, conflict, coincidence and decomposition. While some CBOs may have a very limited objective such as building a defence wall, and once that is achieved, lose momentum, others may develop a wider ideological perspective and go on to struggle for a redistribution of resources and quite wide-ranging social changes. The evolution of any community based mitigation practice, in the context of given political conditions, is a changing relationship between the implementation measures to mitigate specific hazards, the availability of resources, the appropriation of technology and the level of organisation and political consciousness. The CBO itself as the principal focus of social organisation, is the axis around which this relationship evolves.

CBO mitigation practice should not be confused with unaided self-help, though many communities without access to resources are forced to rely on small, makeshift mitigation measures at the local level, which often prove to be totally inadequate against the magnitude of the hazards faced. It is all too easy to romanticise the virtues of traditional techniques and methods, which in themselves may only reflect severe technological and economic constraints and an acute lack of resources. Community based mitigation also means making the state participate: obtaining resources; changing policies and negotiating effective support from central and local government. While some mitigation measures, such as house reinforcement, may be best managed at the community level, large infrastructure works or major policy changes usually require a level of centralised authority and management which only the state possesses. Community based mitigation is not about excluding

"Community based mitigation is about involving governments in supporting communities' own mitigation programmes." Here, a government bulldozer clears up debris from the 1984 huaico in the village of San Jose de Palle in the Rimac Valley, according to plans drawn up by PREDES in consultation with local people.

Andrew Maskrey/Juvenal Medina/Predes

governments. On the contrary, it is about involving governments in supporting communities' own mitigation programmes.

When CBOs are in control of mitigation it is possible to avoid the diseconomies and mismatches which characterise top down programmes. Because CBOs use the undervalued and unrecognised contributions that all groups in the community make (including women, young people and the elderly) they maximise the use of all available local resources as well as making better use of scarce external resources. Community based mitigation can achieve a lot more with a lot less compared to top down programmes. Community based mitigation is not necessarily restricted to small scale measures at the local level. Through coordination and coalition CBOs are able to exercise control over large scale mitigation measures, while retaining the essential match between local needs and actions. In effect, the central resource available for mitigation on any scale is people themselves and only through community based mitigation can that resource be fully utilised.

In conclusion, community based mitigation programmes represent a real opportunity to use disaster as a vehicle for development. Vulnerability is gradually reduced, eliminating the conditions in which new disasters occur. Strengthening community organisation builds self-confidence and enables people to take more control over their situation and seek ways to improve it.

Chapter Ten

IMPLEMENTING COMMUNITY BASED MITIGATION

The Task for NGOs

Supporting people mitigating disaster means working to bring about a policy change from top down mitigation to community based mitigation. NGOs are in the best position to bring about this policy change. They are relatively autonomous, not dependent on the government or on market forces, so they can act as third parties between CBOs and governments. Their role is to act as an enabler and adviser to CBOs in the implementation of mitigation programmes. Because each situation is different, there are no standardised procedures to be followed, but from the experiences already described it is possible to draw out a number of principles and practices which may be useful to NGOs and others wishing to encourage community based mitigation.

1. Identifying CBOs

In areas where community organisations already exist, NGOs can work through them. Where no local organisation exists or where existing organisations are unable to respond to the disaster situation, then NGOs may need to stimulate new forms of organisation (such as emergency committees or reconstruction committees). Such organisations often turn into fully fledged CBOs through the experience of working together in the disaster context. NGOs should take care, however, not to stimulate the formation of special sectorial organisations for mitigation in a way that weakens or divides existing community organisations and structures.

2. Strengthening CBOs

Organisation is the key element in community based mitigation. The level of organisation which people possess, its effectiveness and people's consciousness of the problems to be tackled are all factors which influence the success of a project. Perhaps the primary role of NGOs supporting community based mitigation programmes is to encourage and build up the organisational process within the community group. NGOs can provide training and advice on methods and procedures for effective organisation

3. Identifying Needs and Priorities

In community based mitigation, the identification of needs and priorities, and thus the character and objectives of each programme, will be made by the CBO or CBOs concerned. In many contexts where generalised vulnerability is very high, mitigation may not be the top priority for the CBOs. Securing land titles, drinking water supply or other services may be more pressing needs. When disaster occurs and mitigation becomes the principal priority for CBOs, NGOs already working in an area prior to a disaster will be in the best position to take the opportunity to deepen their working relationships with CBOs and stimulate innovation and change. Enabling CBOs to carry out successful mitigation programmes can be a means of stimulating and encouraging them to take on a wider development role.

4. Developing Proposals

CBOs may have clear objectives and goals, but be unclear about the technical, legal and financial measures available to attain the goals. One of the principal contributions of NGOs is to develop mitigation proposals, which CBOs can adopt as their own. In this way, people's implicit demands, both for mitigation and for housing and other services, can be expressed in terms of viable projects and programmes, which can be negotiated with government and other agencies.

The development of proposals involves integrating a range of factors: geological, ecological, social, economic and so on. Proposals must balance different needs and priorities and not just consist of technically viable solutions to mitigating the effects of a given hazard. Planning should be an incremental process and proposals should increase in comprehensiveness as people's understanding and awareness increases. At each stage, the possibility of implementation both in technical as well as political and economic terms, should closely match what is being proposed. NGOs can have a clear advisory role to CBOs in the process of formulating proposals, carrying out research or passing on the results of existing research or experience.

Luke Holland/Oxfam
By working through community based organisations, people's needs can be prioritised. In some situations, securing adequate supplies of clean water may be seen as even more important than disaster mitigation.

5. Encouraging Participation

The participation of people in the analysis of problems and the development of proposals is a vital characteristic of community based mitigation. The starting point is always the specific problems a community faces and people's perceptions of how to solve them. Proposals must be developed gradually, step-by-step. While this is a long process, in which each element has to be discussed and approved laboriously in meetings, it avoids the difficulties which can arise when proposals are generated outside, do not coincide with local needs and demands and overlook conflicting interests and objectives within the community. The long process of achieving consensus is worthwhile as it results in better proposals and a stronger community organisation

6. Providing Technical Assistance

Implementing mitigation in a way that reinforces community organisation requires the development of appropriate tools. NGOs should work with CBOs to develop mitigation tools which maximise the use of local resources and which are susceptible to local control. Effective mitigation is more often made up of the accumulation of a large number of locally diverse solutions, rather than one large scale, standardised measure. In most areas, vulnerability is so complex that there is no single, simple solution.

Through appropriate tools, community based mitigation can achieve an efficiency and an economy which is denied to top down programmes. Scarce outside resources can then be applied where they are really needed. Apart from technologies for flood defence or seismic resistant building, tools can also include, for example, local systems for managing credit and external funding, legal mechanisms which give the community control over land and services and organisational structures for managing and implementing projects. These tools must then be developed through practice, failures and successes identified and modifications made.

7. Learning from Experience

When tools have been developed they can then be shared more widely through training courses and through the production of training materials. NGOs should help CBOs to learn from experience. This learning should be a process of reflection not only on problems faced and ways of overcoming them but also on the internal structure of the organisation, its relationship with the community and with the state and other agencies. There are many different popular education methods which NGOs can use in this way. The method used will depend on each specific situation. Organisation workshops, training manuals and information materials in different formats, community theatre, local media can all be effective ways of communicating knowledge and sharing skills

8. Building Networks

Local NGOs must take on the responsibility of transferring and sharing methods and tools with other groups so that a real process of horizontal learning can take place, with an exchange of information and the perfection and improvement of methodology and tools. In order to exchange methods and tools, NGOs with experience in supporting CBO mitigation programmes must form networks by setting up communication channels between NGOs.

Community based programmes which need to cover large populations in large geographical areas can do so through the incremental clustering of small programmes, with a commonly agreed framework of objectives. Networks of local CBOs operating within a common set of objectives, have implemented very large programmes, without losing essential local specificity. The principal of incremental growth means that programmes should always start small and evolve gradually, incorporating new CBOs and geographical areas over time.

It is important that NGOs respect the style of community organisation in the areas where they work and understand the impact of external political and economic forces on that style. NGOs should work gradually, building up the confidence of existing CBOs, before trying to encourage the formation of larger scale organisations. All the NGO should do is provide opportunities for contact and cooperation and offer advice. It cannot and should not direct the process.

9. Negotiating with Governments

NGOs can help CBOs formulate their demands clearly and present them to government and international agencies. A CBO which has a coherent picture of the aid it actually requires to carry out its own proposals is in a qualitatively different position from CBOs which are merely passive recipients of relief. Groups of CBO's can negotiate more effectively with governments and other agencies. At first, NGOs may need to accompany CBOs in negotiating with government departments, but as the CBO grows in confidence and effectiveness, responsibility for such negotiations should be taken over entirely by the CBO.

10. Using Disaster Relief Aid

A critical factor in most disasters is the existence of and use made of relief aid. It is all too often assumed that successful response to disaster is measured by the volume of aid donated and received. Experience, however, seems to demonstrate the contrary. External relief aid often retards and inhibits processes of autonomous local development and fails to respond to people's real needs and demands. The way relief is distributed and used seems to be far more important than how much of it there is.

A key decision to be faced by NGOs supporting community based mitigation programmes is how to deal with the relief aid that often floods into an area after a large disaster. Firstly, NGOs must recognise that recovery and rehabilitation does not just depend on relief. The existence of strong community organisation, of appropriate tools and viable proposals, are factors that have far more weight. In general, most real mitigation depends more on changing existing policy and on resolving problems in an area than it does on receiving emergency relief. However, when relief is channelled through and controlled by CBOs it can act as a catalyst for local organisation and development.

It is important that NGOs are not perceived by CBOs as relief and donor agencies. If that perception arises it tends to negate the kind of relationship which is required to be able to enable and advise community based mitigation programmes. When NGOs administer relief aid for international agencies, it should be channelled through CBOs. Food aid can be used to support work programmes, for example, rather than immobilise community initiatives, as too often happens. Relief aid should be used sparingly. Too much is usually more damaging than too little.

11. Integrating Mitigation with Development

Because they must respond to CBOs' own needs and demands, programmes must strive to be multisectorial in terms of content and timespan. The best programmes are those which integrate all phases of disaster (preparation; emergency; recovery; reconstruction) and different sectors (housing; agriculture; infrastructure and so on), without losing the specificity of skills of the NGO. All the evidence shows that people themselves do not divide their lives into sectors, and even though unisectorial, top down programmes may be easy to manage for large agencies, they rarely respond to people's real needs.

The integration of mitigation with other tasks which CBOs face is a key to ensuring that the stimulus provided by the disaster carries over into long term development activity, which can reduce vulnerability.

NGOs can also help by acting as guarantors for aid given to CBOs by using their bank account and legal status on the CBOs' behalf. Such arrangements permit the organisation of community credit schemes and revolving funds, which allow funds for emergency relief to be used for development activities.

12. Forming Coalitions

Pilot projects supported by NGOs can serve to demonstrate alternative policy options for disaster mitigation, which can then be adopted by central and local government and by international agencies. NGOs should take on the responsibility of documenting and making explicit these alternatives in the form of plans, policies, concepts and principles for mitigation. In Mexico, for example, after the 1985 earthquake a pilot project, implemented by a local NGO, served as a model for a large scale government reconstruction project after the disaster.

Usually, however, NGOs must form coalitions in order to bring pressure to bear on external agencies. Coalitions can be built up on the basis of existing networks to present the results of research and of experience to governments and agencies and to press for policy changes.

An Agenda for the Agencies

Bilateral and multilateral aid agencies also have a large responsibility and a fundamental role to play in bringing about a policy change from top down to community based mitigation programmes. Many agencies still have a far greater commitment to emergency relief than to mitigation, while most mitigation programmes still have a top down approach. It is vital that agencies change their role from managers of top down mitigation programmes to enablers of community based mitigation programmes. Redirecting even a small percentage of their funds towards supporting CBO mitigation programmes could have a dramatic and positive effect on the occurrence of disasters in the future.

Channelling international aid into top down programmes, whether emergency relief programmes or reconstruction programmes, is neither cost effective nor efficient, nor does it catalyse development. Aid frequently does not reach the intended beneficiaries, does not respond to their real needs and creates dependency, leaving people more vulnerable than before the disaster

From Disaster Relief to Development

In general, agencies should put less emphasis on material aid for disaster and more emphasis on supporting the enabling and advisory activities of local NGOs. Agencies should commit funds to supporting pilot mitigation programmes carried out by CBOs with the support of local NGOs. At the same time, agencies should recognise that when material aid is channelled through CBOs, with local NGOs acting as guarantors, emergency relief can become an effective way of catalysing community based mitigation programmes which lead to the long term reduction of vulnerability. Such aid can become a very effective tool for development.

By changing their approach in this way agencies could do a great deal more with a great deal less. All the case studies analysed in this paper show that the quantity of aid which is given is a great deal less important than the way it is used. CBOs and the local NGOs that support them have an incomparable efficiency, not only in the distribution of aid but in its use to stimulate the reinforcement of organisation, technical innovation and the implementation of mitigation measures in practice.

The change in approach also means that international agencies must work through local NGOs, wherever possible. Unfortunately, many agencies still prefer to implement their own projects directly, even though competent local organisations may exist. However, in many contexts there are no effective local NGOs. A key responsibility of the agencies is to build up local capacity where it does not exist and to support and reinforce it where it does. In the same way that NGOs must seek to build up greater levels of community organisation, in order to avoid creating dependency, agencies must build up local NGO capacity, establishing their own role as an international support and enabler.

In order to achieve this change in approach agencies must modify their own concepts of disaster. The programmes of many agencies still demonstrate the 'dominant' approach to disaster (seeing disasters as inevitable results of the action of natural forces on people and their activities) and operating within tight and limited definitions of what disaster relief and mitigation are. The result is that funds are only released for short term relief or reconstruction projects. Agencies must broaden their project categories to enable CBO mitigation programmes to be considered as 'disaster' programmes so that disaster funds can be used to support long term mitigation programmes both after and, most importantly, before disasters occur. There is still little or no concern with pre-disaster planning despite the fact that all the evidence demonstrates its enormous importance.

Supporting Networks

Another area in which agencies should play a key role and where their activity is currently negligible is in stimulating NGO networks in order to build up a real exchange of methods and tools for disaster mitigation. Very little systematic use is made of project experiences, even by those agencies which implement projects directly. Agencies should insist that NGOs produce training materials and comparative case studies from their own experiences. They should also stimulate the formation of networks, through the organising of seminars and the financing of newsletters and information exchanges. A relatively small investment by agencies in these activities could produce significant improvements in the effectiveness of community based mitigation programmes. Agencies have a particular responsibility to encourage local NGOs to incorporate mitigation as an element within their development programmes.

Similarly, agencies should be more willing to support the production, publication and dissemination of research based on project and programme experiences and which demonstrate policy options for governments, NGOs and agencies themselves. Many NGOs, which could play a decisive role in disaster mitigation, still have a very narrow understanding of disaster, seeing it as isolated from social process, and are unaware of their own potential for intervention.

By supporting networking activities agencies can:

- **generate and stimulate new pilot projects at the local level**
- **build up the range of methods and tools available for community based disaster mitigation**
- **encourage the formulation of policy options by coalitions of NGOs working together on different themes.**

At present, stimulating the formation of national, regional and international networks of NGOs is the single most important task which agencies must put on their own agendas for action.

FURTHER READING

WINCHESTER, Peter, *Vulnerability and Recovery in Hazard Prone Areas*, Middle East and Mediterranean Regional Conference on Earthen and Low Strength Masonry Buildings in Seismic Areas: Middle East Technical University, Ankara, Turkey, August, 1986.

CUNY, Fred, *Disasters and Development*, Oxford University Press, 1983.

HEWITT, Kenneth, 'The Idea of Calamity in a Technocratic Age', Chapter 1 in *Interpretations of Calamity*, Allen & Unwin, 1983.

WATTS, Michael, 'On the Poverty of Theory: Natural Hazards Research, in Context', Chapter 13 in *Interpretations of Calamity*, Allen & Unwin, 1983.

SUSMAN, O'KEEFE, WISNER, 'Global Disasters. A Radical Interpretation', Chapter 4 in *Interpretations of Catastrophe*, Allen & Unwin 1983.

DAVIS, Ian, 'A Critical Review of the Work Method and Findings of the Housing and Natural Hazards Group', *International Karakorum Project*, Cambridge University Press, 1984.

MASKREY, Andrew, ROMERO, Gilberto, *Como Entender los Desastres Naturales*, PREDES, Lima, Peru, August 1983.

DAVIS, Ian, 'Disasters as Agents of Change', *Habitat International* Vol. 7, 1983.

DAVIS, Ian, *Basic Elements for a National Model of Disaster Management and an Examination of Comparative Models of National Disaster Management*, Symposium Manejo Particiativo de Calamidades Publicas, Bogota, Colombia, 1985.

DAVIS, Ian, 'Prevention is Better Than Cure', *RRDC Bulletin*, October 1984.

MASKREY, Andrew, *Community Based Hazard Mitigation*, International Conference on Natural Hazard Mitigation Programme Implementation, Ocho Rios, Jamaica, November 1984.

NORTON, Reggie, 'Disasters and Settlements', *Disasters* Vol.4 No.3, 1980.

LEWIS, James, *Disaster Mitigation planning: Some Lessons from Island Countries*, University of Bath, 1985.

WISNER, O'KEEFE, WESTAGE, 'Global Systems and Local Disasters: The Untapped Power of People's Science', *Disasters*, Vol.1 No.1 1977.

DAVIS, I. *Making Use of Disasters to Advance Mitigation*, International Converence on Disaster Mitigation Programme Implementation, Jamaica, 1984.

MUMTAZ, Baber, *Mitigation in the Context of Development*, International Conference on Disaster Mitigation Programme Implementation, Jamaica, 1984.